al sensitivity, Carroll helps us understand not only the
n but also how it brings us face-to-face with the cruci-
Taking us beyond polemical debates, he examines our
l faith and the gift and challenges of the reign of God.
.nore of a classic in studies in theology and migration, it
calls us to see the God who migrated to us in the Incarnation and in turn invites us to a
homeward journey marked by compassion and solidarity."

—**Daniel G. Groody, CSC**, University of Notre Dame

"Immigration is one of the most urgent issues affecting the church in the United States
today. *Christians at the Border* challenges Christ-followers to address the topic, first and
foremost, as Christians committed to the authority of Scripture. Daniel Carroll combines
thorough analysis of the biblical texts related to immigrants and immigration with a deep,
personal understanding of the many ways that immigration affects people made in God's
image. Every Christian seeking an informed, biblical understanding of this complex topic
should read this book."

—**Matthew Soerens**, US church training specialist, World Relief;
coauthor of *Welcoming the Stranger: Justice, Compassion,
and Truth in the Immigration Debate*

"As Christians, our decisions about politics, ministry to the afflicted, and church engagement must begin with a thorough biblical study on the subject. This book sets the biblical
foundation for understanding the issue of immigration, so that we start from the same
point as together we explore difficult questions about this issue. The second edition also
includes examples of how some evangelical communities are applying these biblical implications. Carroll's book is a tool for communities who are seeking to first ask the right
questions and then fulfill the Great Commandment and the Great Commission with the
immigrants among us. Thank you, *hermanito*!"

—**Alejandro (Alex) Mandes**, executive director, Immigrant Hope,
immigranthope.org

"As a Christian who cares about justice and the church's ministry to immigrants living in
our nation, I am so grateful for Danny Carroll's book, *Christians at the Border*, which
offers a biblical and compelling case for God's concern for those on the margins of society.
A must-read!"

—**Noel Castellanos**, CEO, Christian Community
Development Association (CCDA)

"*Christians at the Border* dialogues fairly with other views and offers a sensitive and bal-
anced call to Christian ethics on immigration. The book both examines direct commands
in Scripture and highlights biblical models and principles, the same way that nineteenth-
century biblical abolitionists argued their case for justice."

—**Craig Keener**, Asbury Theological Seminary

"This book is a must-read for pastors and parishioners and also for politicians and policy-
makers. The cry for justice that echoes through the pages of the Bible resounds afresh
through the scholarly care with which Danny Carroll makes his compelling case in *Christians at the Border*. Just and comprehensive immigration reform remains an urgent and
pressing concern in the United States and beyond, and Carroll nourishes the debate with
a clear and convincing analysis of the biblical imperatives that call for the church to be
firm in its advocacy on behalf of our immigrant sisters and brothers."

—**Jean-Pierre Ruiz**, St. John's University, New York

Praise for the First Edition

"With a foot in both cultures and a sensitivity to the arguments of all sides, Carroll presents *Christians at the Border* to sort through the complicated and confusing immigration debate with nuance. He goes further than many studies by examining the question with a theological and biblical eye, a factor frequently ignored in what is often a shrill debate. Perspective is what such a complicated discussion requires, and that is what this book delivers. Read and learn."

—**Darrell Bock**, Dallas Theological Seminary

"Danny Carroll's goal of providing Christians with a biblical and theological framework to participate in the US immigration debate *as Christians* is met brilliantly in *Christians at the Border*. He addresses both the complexities of the issues related to migration in a globalized world—within the specific history of the United States—and the broader biblical perspective that begins with the reality that all humans are created in the image of God. Even as he acknowledges that the Bible does not give us a specific policy blueprint, he demonstrates that Scripture provides important and clear principles that allow us to address the issue from a Christian perspective."

—**Juan Francisco Martínez**, Fuller Theological Seminary

"Combining prophetic zeal with a tender, pastoral tone, Professor Carroll calls on Christians to adopt a distinctively Christian disposition to the issue of undocumented immigrants and even more importantly to the *people* who find themselves in this situation. He argues convincingly that for Christians, the ethic of compassion and commitment to the well-being of the marginalized must take precedence over legality. If we heed his plea, immigrants will know when they encounter us that they have crossed the border into a land of distinctively gracious people."

—**Daniel I. Block**, Wheaton College Graduate School

"Danny Carroll R. has the kind of scholarly background in biblical studies and cultural anthropology that the subject calls for. He articulates well the facts, questions, and perspectives. He proposes answers, or at least gives suggestions, that are both compassionate and realistic, and he does so from a soundly biblical and distinctly Christian point of view. But this is not just a well-researched book. The author has both personal history and experience that make him the right person to approach the current immigration issues in a penetrating and sympathetic way. This man and his book deserve serious consideration in the current debate."

—**Richard E. Averbeck**, Trinity Evangelical Divinity School

"[Carroll] brings his professional expertise and personal heritage to this brief examination of Hispanic immigration, a hot topic in the current political climate, in light of the Bible. . . . This brief treatment is an excellent addition to the literature of biblical theology and a valuable contribution to the debates on immigration in this country. Highly recommended for academic libraries, particularly those with intercultural or religious studies."

—**Ray Arnett**, *Library Journal*

"This well-argued and carefully researched study draws on biblical precedent to construct a viable Christian ethic on contemporary immigration. Carroll . . . focuses primarily on Hispanic immigration to the U.S. in his examples, though the theological discussions are applicable on a broad intercultural level. He explores biblical notions of the responsibility an ancient society had to assist sojourners and those in exile, attempting to move today's discourse about immigration away from political and racial ideology toward what he hopes is 'a divine viewpoint.' Though Carroll's approach is substantive, even scholarly, the book is surprisingly accessible in language and tone."

—*Publishers Weekly*

Second Edition

christians

at the

border

Immigration, the Church, and the Bible

m. daniel carroll r.

BrazosPress

a division of Baker Publishing Group
Grand Rapids, Michigan

Published by Brazos Press
a division of Baker Publishing Group
P.O. Box 6287, Grand Rapids, MI 49516-6287
www.brazospress.com

Printed in the United States of America

Library of Congress Cataloging-in-Publication Data is on file at the Library of Congress, Washington, DC.

ISBN 978-1-58743-351-1 (pbk.)

13   14   15   16   17   18   19   7   6   5   4   3   2   1

In keeping with biblical principles of creation stewardship, Baker Publishing Group advocates the responsible use of our natural resources. As a member of the Green Press Initiative, our company uses recycled paper when possible. The text paper of this book is composed in part of post-consumer waste.

Al pueblo hispano—
peregrinos en tierra ajena,
artesanos de una vida nueva,
semilla de esperanza—
paz y ánimo para el largo camino

To the Christian church in the United States:
may we never forget that we are
sojourners in a strange land,
and that among us
there is neither Jew nor Greek

Contents

Foreword

Samuel Rodríguez

*National Hispanic
Christian Leadership Conference*

As Christians our faith stands universally recognized by a simple symbol, a cross. The cross is both vertical and horizontal. Vertically we stand connected to God, his kingdom, eternal truth, and glory. Horizontally, to our left and to our right, we stand connected to family, culture, society, and community.

Immigration reform is both a vertical and horizontal issue. Vertically, the heart of God stands moved by the plight of immigrants and their suffering. Horizontally, passing immigration reform will serve as a reconciliatory prescription for a nation divided by partisan politics.

Accordingly, it is the cross that prompts us to lift our hands toward heaven and to stretch our hands toward our neighbor. It is the cross that enables us to see the image of God in citizen and immigrant. It is the cross that compels us to declare that a human being cannot be illegal. It is the cross that drives us to reconcile the rule of law (Rom. 13) with treating the immigrant as one of our own (Lev. 19).

In *Christians at the Border*, Daniel Carroll Rodas, the national immigration spokesperson for the National Hispanic Christian Leadership Conference, calls on those foundational elements of our society in order to address the issue of immigration from a biblical, historical, economic, and kingdom perspective. He succeeds in contextualizing the immigration issue and transforming the platform from a debate to a dialogue, particularly among Americans and certainly among fellow Christians.

As Danny has represented our 40,118 member churches in White House, congressional, and regional meetings, and as I have found myself traveling from California to Washington, DC, weekly for over two years, attempting to broker a viable compromise on this issue, three fundamental questions arose. First, how should Christians respond to the immigration issue? Second, what do Americans, and especially American Christians, need to know in order to respond in a manner consistent with our Judeo-Christian value system? And finally—the question raised by reporters, members of Congress, senators, and White House staffers—does the Bible provide any guidance on the issue of immigration? *Christians at the Border* offers answers to these questions. This book will help the majority culture and Hispanics begin to think about and respond to this issue primarily as Christians and citizens of God's kingdom. Without a doubt, Carroll offers the theological and biblical framework in which the followers of Jesus Christ can analyze, evaluate, and act in respect to immigration, and to the Hispanic immigrant community in particular, in a manner that complements the ethos of our Christian journey.

It is impossible to have a thorough understanding of the current immigration discussion without taking into consideration the dynamics of the three-legged stool upon which the future of immigration in America rests: cultural identity, economic impact, and Hispanic Christianity. Carroll begins the journey of framing the biblical approach toward immigration by describing the socio-ethno convergence of these three driving forces in an unbiased, objective, and sound manner. As a result, Christians committed to a transformational missiology will be better equipped to address the issues of cultural identity, assimilation, economic impact, and global ramifications with sound biblical support. Certainly, the most intriguing fact stemming from the data presented by Professor Carroll addresses the opportunities that exist both for America and, more importantly, for God's kingdom. I wholeheartedly believe that by the time readers finish *Christians at the Border*, their approach will change from debating the immigration issue to discussing the immigration opportunity.

Tangentially, it is important to note that, as America's fastest-growing religious demographic, Hispanic Christ followers stand poised to reconcile the optics of redemption with the metrics of reconciliation. This community full of purpose, passion, and promise carries the anointing to preserve biblical orthodoxy, ignite a righteousness and justice movement, edify a firewall of holiness and humility, and project a kingdom-culture multi-ethnic demonstration of the gospel, all through the power of the Holy Spirit.

To that end, Danny's application of both vertical and horizontal optics takes us on a journey from Genesis to the New Testament in order to extrapolate biblical principles and truths pertaining to the immigrant community. In a persuasive, logical, and systematic fashion, *Christians at the Border* enables the reader to view the immigrant as a sojourner. Furthermore, this book strengthens the historical role of America's faith communities, offering them a foundation to act in the spirit of reconciliation by exposing the nexus of compassion and the rule of law within an enriching canopy both for our nation and for the kingdom of God.

Finally, we cannot deny the fact that the immigration issue has the potential of either polarizing our society or enriching our narrative. My hope is for the latter. A hope that the spirit of compassion, love, and tolerance stemming from the Judeo-Christian ethos and embedded in our collective narrative will once again prevail and embrace righteousness and justice for all. A hope that the Christian community will rise up, speak vociferously from the pulpit of reconciliation to all corridors of our society, and demand an end to extreme ideologies from all sides of this debate.

We must recognize that at the various crossroads of American history, when despair and desperation coalesced around the inevitable defeat of reason, oracles of truth arose to articulate and disseminate to the masses the moral imperative of sound, practical, and graceful deliberation. From the Revolutionary War to the abolitionist movement to the struggle for civil rights in the 1960s, writers, scholars, and clergy have presented the case for truth and righteousness in a way that is compatible with the values of a biblical worldview. In *Christians at the Border*, Professor Carroll continues in that very prophetic and practical role. Undoubtedly, even when—it is no longer a matter of if—legislation is passed that deals with the various dynamics of the immigration debate, the content of this book will serve as a primer on immigration issues for years to come. For at the end of the day, immigration reform does not stem from the agenda of the donkey or the elephant; rather, welcoming the stranger is a conviction that flows from the agenda of the Lamb.

Preface to the
Second Edition

Much has changed since the first edition of *Christians at the Border* appeared in the spring of 2008. At that time, months before President Obama's election to his first term in office, there was hope that immigration would be an important topic of the campaign. There had been a few attempts at legislation reform in the preceding years, and immigration had occupied the media's attention. It seemed as if there was some momentum as election activities heated up. But then . . . nothing. Immigration disappeared from the nation's radar screen. Neither political party wanted to alienate certain sectors of their constituencies.

Little talk about immigration came out of Washington in the first years of the Obama administration, as its efforts centered on a sweeping health care initiative. Immigration eventually re-appeared in the media, however, with continued highly emotive reports and declarations coming from all sides of the debate. Piecemeal measures came from the White House, like the DACA memo (Deferred Action for Childhood Arrivals) in the summer of 2012, which was designed to prevent the removal of qualified undocumented youth, though it did not provide a pathway to legal status. In the election cycle that fall the Hispanic vote and immigration did play a central role, and the Obama reelection seemed to guarantee that immigration reform would become a reality in the near future.

While all this was going on in the political world, something amazing was happening in Christian circles—and this from across the theological spectrum, from the Catholic tradition to mainline and evangelical denominations. Leaders at every level and from all sorts of institutions and ministries were coming together to work for outreach to immigrants in communities across the nation and to advocate for new legislation. Groups that normally do not collaborate were now standing shoulder to shoulder in these efforts.

For me personally, *Christians at the Border* has generated all kinds of writing opportunities and invitations to speak in many venues in different parts of the country. I have had the privilege of witnessing firsthand this new movement of God as I have interacted with Jews, Roman Catholics, and a wide array of Protestant groups. The gracious commitment to the stranger that is coming from so many directions has been an encouragement to those of us trying to effect change.

These experiences and the changing political landscape have led to this second edition. The historical and legal discussion in the first chapter has been updated, as has the appendix. I have added material to the biblical sections and thoroughly reworked the endnotes. In addition, Samuel Rodríguez and Ron Sider kindly revised their foreword and afterword, respectively.

Hopefully, immigration reform soon will become a reality, if it already has not by the time this revision is published. Yet much work will remain. The people of God will need to continue to be informed about the call to welcome the outsider and to grow in divine hospitality. Negative attitudes and fears do not change immediately with legislation. New laws simply provide a broader arena for working out a perspective in our daily lives that will please the Lord we confess to serve. In other words, what is presented in this book will continue to have relevance for some time to come. My hope is that this second edition of *Christians at the Border* will be, as was the first, a helpful resource for orienting Christians toward welcoming the strangers in our midst.

April 2013

Acknowledgments

I would like to thank several individuals for helping make this book, both the first and second editions, a reality. Jim Kinney of Baker Academic listened to my ideas for this book with his usual patience and graciousness and then worked hard to birth the project. I am grateful that he took on its vision of offering to the "ordinary Christian" a more informed reflection on the Hispanic presence within the United States. Jim was receptive to the need for a second edition, which would update the socio-legal data and expand on the biblical foundations of the first, and he has patiently helped see this revision to its completion.

Two outstanding and visionary leaders within the evangelical community have provided the foreword and afterword. Reverend Samuel Rodríguez is president of the National Hispanic Christian Leadership Conference, an association of more than forty thousand Hispanic churches and a wide variety of ministries committed to the Hispanic community. I have had the privilege of serving on the NHCLC board and as its national immigration spokesperson. Ron Sider for many years has been the voice of evangelical social concern and has published widely in the field. He also was the evangelical convener for Catholics and Evangelicals for the Common Good, which consisted of a small group of leaders from both traditions who met for several years to discuss shared convictions on life and justice matters, including the topic of immigration. For this reason, Ron graciously invited me to participate in that dialogue.

Jonathan Jameson and Giles Classen, former students of mine at Denver Seminary, helped me with several facets of the first edition. Kayla White, my graduate assistant, has helped with the search for new materials, the checking of multiple internet sources for this revision, and the index. My older son, Matthew, recommended the powerful photo by Alex Webb for the new cover.

Two Hispanic pastors in the Denver area have been wonderful encouragers, from that original edition until today. Erik Valenzuela, a Guatemalan, and Jorge Barbarán, a Peruvian, were keys to the successful launching of Denver Seminary's Spanish-speaking program, IDEAL (Instituto para el Desarrollo y Adiestramiento de Líderes), where I initially heard the stories of undocumented immigrants. They have been models of ministerial dedication, and I am privileged to call them friends. Erik is my pastor at Iglesia El Camino, and *mis hermanos y hermanas* of that church have welcomed me into their hearts and been open to my questions and ponderings. Federico Maes, a lawyer of Spanish-American descent and an ardent student of the Bible, has amazed me with his boundless energy and deep commitment to our people and the Hispanic church. He, too, is a friend and model, whom the Lord in his grace has allowed to cross my path. I have learned much also from the ministers of the Alianza Ministerial Hispana of metro Denver, who sometimes were not quite sure what to do with a bicultural seminary professor.

Christians at the Border was birthed under Dr. Craig Williford's presidency at Denver Seminary. He was a visionary at the time, moving into the uncharted waters of Hispanic cultural and church life. Not many seminaries possess either the courage or the commitment to serve all for the sake of the kingdom of

God. Our current president, Dr. Mark Young, has affirmed this direction with his call that theological education be missional. It has been a joy to found IDEAL and to turn over the leadership of the seminary's Hispanic initiatives to Wilmer Ramírez, a Honduran and former student of mine from SETECA (Seminario Teológico Centroamericano), the seminary in Guatemala City where I taught for many years before coming to Denver. He and his wife, Vioneth, have advanced the cause of Christ institutionally and in our local Hispanic community in amazing ways.

Finally, I am grateful to my family. To my mother, Edit Rodas Carroll, for having reminded me of the importance of *nuestra guatemalidad*. I am blessed with a wonderful wife, Joan, who has lived with this complex character of mixed heritage for over thirty years. Countless times she has listened patiently to this *Quijote*, who always seems to be on the quest to understand himself and life as a cultural hybrid, and she has been willing to venture continuously across cultural boundaries with me. I only hope that I have been a worthy guide. Our sons, Matthew and Adam, were raised in the two very different worlds of Guatemala and the United States. My prayer is that they continue to learn to admire this country, but never lose *el amor por la patria de su juventud*; that they learn the language of efficiency and technology, but nurture in their souls *el idioma del amor y de los sueños*; and that in their hearts they always find a place for both the eagle and *el quetzal*.*

* The *quetzal* is the national bird of Guatemala.

Introduction

I am the son of a Guatemalan mother and an American father. My parents met in New Orleans after the Second World War, were married in Guatemala, and then moved to the United States. I was born and grew up in Houston, but in many ways my life was different from most.

My mother made a point of raising my brother and me bilingual and bicultural. Speaking both English and Spanish was something natural. Piñatas were the high points of our birthday parties, and *noche buena* (Christmas Eve) was celebrated with tamales and black beans. We frequently had family and friends from Guatemala come through our home, and my parents had several Cuban friends in the area whom we would visit; in time my brother would marry a Cuban woman. As boys, my brother and I spent entire summers in Guatemala. We would stay with family after our parents returned to the US, and during those times we grew to know the country and participated in Latin American culture in many ways. During several summers our parents enrolled us in a school called La Preparatoria (the Guatemalan academic year runs from mid-January to mid-October). The school was located in front of the central post office in downtown Guatemala City and was not far from the coffee shop our grandmother owned, across the street from the national palace. At noon, when classes would break for a couple of hours (a Latin American tradition that has almost completely disappeared because of the size of cities today), we would walk from school to Le Petit Café and then go on to our grandmother's house for lunch before heading back to classes in the afternoon.

A decade later things changed drastically from those more halcyon days. There was a massive earthquake in 1976. The school we had attended was one of the buildings destroyed, and my grandmother's neighborhood was forever changed. I, too, was now a different person. I had finished college, where I had come to a personal faith in Christ. I also was recently married and a first-year seminary student. But even harsher times lay ahead for Guatemala.

After seminary my wife and I moved to Guatemala in the summer of 1982. This was during the troubled presidency of Efraín Ríos Montt. Since the early 1960s, Guatemala had been in an armed conflict, but the war escalated over time to horrific proportions and was at its most violent just before our arrival. The rest of the isthmus was also in turmoil. The hostilities in El Salvador were at their peak; the Sandinistas were in power in Nicaragua, and the Contras were seeking to oust them. A peace treaty between the Guatemalan government and the guerrilla forces would eventually be signed in December 1996, but by then the fighting had taken untold thousands of lives and left many more widowed, orphaned, and displaced.[1]

During that fascinating yet tragic time, we raised our family in the capital city, where I taught at El Seminario Teológico Centroamericano (SETECA). After fifteen years there, we returned to the United States, and I assumed a position at Denver Seminary. I continue, however, as an adjunct at SETECA, so I am able to be in our beloved Guatemala every year to teach and spend time with friends and family in that world so profoundly rooted in my soul.

The war changed Guatemala in many ways, some of which are inseparably connected to the topic of this book. Many left the country—some fleeing political persecution, others merely looking for a new start, one with the promise of a better and more peaceful life. The United States was the natural destination for most. Since the end of that conflict, international economic realities have attracted even more Guatemalans to the US. Of course, millions from Mexico and other Latin American countries have made their way north, too.

A Unique Perspective?

North America is changing and will never be the same. Spanish-speaking television networks (Univisión, Telemundo) are growing in influence; Latin American cuisine is becoming standard fare in many parts; music on the radio (and all sorts of handheld devices) is rocking to different beats, and the Latin Grammy Awards is an annual event; Jennifer López, Salma Hayek, Antonio Banderas, and other actors cross over between English- and Spanish-speaking roles; Latin Americans (players, managers, and now owners) dominate baseball, and soccer (*fútbol*) is gaining in popularity; Spanish newspapers and magazines are springing up everywhere; the Hispanic Chamber of Commerce wields growing clout locally and nationally; Hispanic voters are impacting elections in major ways, and both houses of Congress have Hispanic members; the premier sports network ESPN also has ESPN Deportes; any number of universities have Chicano or Latino/a departments and immigration research centers; many neighborhoods and shopping areas are taking on a new look; Cinco de Mayo celebrations are growing; the color of the work force is changing—the list could go on. "The 25 Most Influential Hispanics in America" was the cover story of the August 22, 2005, issue of *Time*, and countless other national magazines and local newspapers have carried reports and editorials on Hispanic immigration during the last few years.

What many fail to realize, however, is that most people of Hispanic descent are not newly arrived immigrants. Millions have been here for generations, and a multitude like myself are of mixed heritage. It is the *recent* surge in the numbers of Hispanics resulting from immigration that has generated unease.

I watch this seismic shift with great interest. My personal background and experience give me something of a distinctive point of view with respect to the complicated situation that is the immigration of Hispanics—more particularly, of undocumented Hispanics—into the United States. I grew up in this country, but

**Too often discussions default
to the passionate ideological
arguments, economic wrangling,
or racial sentiments that
dominate national discourse.**

always with a foot south of the border. A sizeable part of my professional life has been exercised in Guatemala (along with travel to many other Central and South American countries), and my research and writing often grow out of my passion for things Latin American and Hispanic. I feel equally comfortable in both English and Spanish, whether speaking, reading, or writing, and my heart and palate swing easily between both worlds. I teach a full load in English at Denver Seminary, but I also played a part in establishing the Spanish-speaking training program there (IDEAL: Instituto para el Desarrollo y Adiestramiento de Líderes). My wife and I attend an Anglo church on Sunday mornings and a Hispanic congregation in the afternoons, and for several years I have served on the steering committee of the Alianza Ministerial Hispana (Hispanic Ministers Alliance) of metro Denver. I also am on the board of the National Hispanic Leadership Conference and function as its national spokesperson on immigration.

In many ways, then, I stand between the majority culture and the Hispanic culture. I care for both, although I must admit my deepest longings are for my Guatemalan roots. My desire, though, is that what follows may speak in constructive ways to both sides of the divide. I do not stand in a neutral place, but I will strive to offer a fresh look at the national debate.

The Purpose of This Book

I am an Old Testament scholar by training, and I am also committed to the mission of the Christian church. For that reason, I am concerned about how the Bible can orient the way the broader Christian community, denominations, local churches, and individual Christians understand their identity and role in the world today. The immigration of undocumented Hispanics is one area to which all must respond, and, of course, millions of these immigrants make some claim to Christian faith.

The topic is huge and extraordinarily complicated. This book tries to do justice to the complexity of the current state of affairs, but I do not pretend to offer solutions to the myriad of contested issues or to propose some sort of legislative cure-all for the many problems. An appreciation of how thorny the situation is, though, can help move us beyond the entrenched posturing and simplistic positions that can characterize the media and politics. It should spur us all to seek a deeper wisdom, and herein lies the purpose of this book.

My intention is to try to move Christians to reconsider their starting point in the immigration debate. Too often discussions default to passionate ideological arguments, economic wrangling, or racial sentiments that pervade the national discourse. In the past there was little awareness among Christians of what might be a divine viewpoint on immigration. In fact, the percentage of those who grounded their positions on their faith is shockingly low.[2] Fortunately, the landscape is changing. Many denominations have taken stances that support reform, and all kinds of groups are sponsoring conferences and producing literature that call for openness toward outsiders. This book is a modest attempt to provide a solid foundation for a truly Christian perspective on immigration. It is neither exhaustive nor comprehensive. Rather, it is designed as a primer for a more biblically and theologically informed approach to the issue of immigration.

The first chapter briefly surveys the history of Hispanic migration to the United States. It then articulates two of the main points of contention concerning undocumented immigrants—the potential impact on both national identity and economics—but it adds relevant observations to each point that usually do not receive the attention they deserve. The chapter closes with another side of Hispanic life that at times is ignored but that should be fundamental to a Christian approach: the role of religion. Hispanic Christian churches, both Protestant and Catholic, are growing and vibrant. They are part of a worldwide trend of migrations that holds profound implications for the future of the Christian faith.

This turn to faith serves as a transition to the next three chapters, which are the heart of the book. Chapters 2 and 3 expound the material in the Old Testament that is pertinent to immigration. Chapter 4 attends to the New Testament's contribution. The biblical material has important things to say to Christians of both the majority and Hispanic cultures. All people from the Christian heritage can gather around this sacred Word, which they share, and listen to the voice of God. Christians must think about and act on Hispanic immigration *as Christians*.

This book is not an academic tome full of specialist jargon and bewildering charts. After each discussion of what the Bible has to offer on the topic, there is a section titled "Implications for Today." These sections are designed to stimulate thinking about how to apply the teachings of the relevant biblical material to the challenges of immigration. The endnotes direct the reader to additional data regarding social, economic, and political issues and biblical research. They are not at the level of a technical monograph, but they can be a helpful beginning for those who desire more information.

The appendix is designed to be a resource tool. It contains several selected bibliographies and lists a number of relevant websites. The index can help the reader quickly find topics, names, and biblical references used in the body of the book and in the endnotes. All in all, my hope is that *Christians at the Border* will be both informative and useful.

Defining Terms

What makes this discussion a bit more controversial is that the label *Hispanic* itself is contested by many. The word originally comes from *Hispania*, an ancient name for the Iberian Peninsula. In more formal Spanish, *hispano* can still refer to things related to Spain. For example, Latin America (Mexico, Central and South America) is also called *Hispanoamérica*. In the United States, however, the term *Hispanic* came into common parlance as a category designation used by the Census Bureau for all people who are of Spanish or Latin American descent. This very broad category lumped together those from different countries, races, national histories, and even languages.[3] For this reason, not a few academics and activists eschew the term altogether as imprecise and an unjust imposition. They prefer the term *Latino* (feminine *Latina*). I certainly sympathize with this concern, but nonetheless I have decided to use Hispanic. This is the word most people are familiar with and the one regularly used in the media. My choice, therefore, is one of convenience and strategy: most readers of this book will be more familiar with the label Hispanic than with Latino.[4]

It also is helpful to distinguish between the terms *refugee* and *immigrant*. Refugees are those persons who have fled their country of origin out of fear of persecution because of their race, religion, social standing, or political views, or those who have escaped an armed conflict.[5] As these people seek another country where they can settle, they can also be called asylum seekers. Due to the violence in Central and South America from the 1970s to the 1990s, large numbers sought asylum or refugee status in the United States, Canada, Europe, and elsewhere. Today, the major source of refugees looking for a new home is Africa. Thousands upon thousands are running away from hostilities in countries such as the Sudan and Somalia. Many are housed in large camps, where they can be confined for years as they wait for sanctuary. The unrest across the Middle East also has generated large refugee populations. The United Nations coordinates aid to these camps and the placement of some to potential host countries through its High Commission for Refugees.

Immigrants, in contrast, are those who have moved to another country of their own volition and are usually seeking lengthy or permanent residence. Immigrants can enter either legally—through official ports of entry and according to the rules of the admissions policies established by the host country—or not. Those who have come into the United States by other means are frequently called illegal aliens.

I prefer the word *undocumented* rather than *illegal* for several reasons. *Illegal* can carry a pejorative connotation, suggesting by definition that the person is guilty of some act, has few scruples, and is prone to civil disobedience. This is not the case with the overwhelming majority of Hispanic immigrants. Most would gladly regularize their status with the government, but the existing system simply does not provide appropriate avenues to do so. What these people have lacked is the proper documentation required by Washington and the workplace. They are not criminals. At the same time, the common label *alien* can evoke the sense of someone unchangeably foreign and other, without hope of reconciliation or mediation. *Illegal aliens*, therefore, is unhelpfully prejudicial. *Undocumented immigrants* is a more just label and better represents the present reality. These people and the national response to their entry and presence are the focus of this book.

An Exhortation to the Reader

The title *Christians at the Border* is a double entendre. In a very real sense everyone in the United States has to take a political position about what is going on at the physical boundary with Mexico. Consciously or unconsciously, we all take a stand at that literal border, a stand that reflects our social, economic, and racial attitudes and situations. But for Christians there is an additional border. It is a metaphorical decision point. We must determine whether the place we choose to stand in the national debate will be based on the Word of God or whether we will ignore its teaching and defend our opinion on other grounds. This border, in other words, confronts us as a crossroads of faith and conviction.

> *Qué el Señor nos ilumine y otorgue entendimiento.*
> May the Lord illumine us and grant us understanding.

Hispanic Immigration

Invasion or Opportunity?

On a steamy night in May 2003, over seventy men, women, and children crammed into a semitrailer in Harlingen, Texas. They were on their way to a new life, and many looked forward to being reunited with loved ones who had preceded them to the United States. But soon that semitrailer became a suffocating inferno. Nineteen died from heat exhaustion and suffocation in what some call "the worst immigrant tragedy in American history."[1]

Detectives John Bishop and Donald Young were working off duty as security at a baptismal party in a Hispanic neighborhood in Denver on May 8, 2005. Suddenly, what should have been a joyous celebration turned grisly. Raúl Gómez García shot both officers in the back, wounding Bishop and killing Young. Gómez García quickly fled the scene and made his way to Mexico. With the cooperation of law enforcement officials there, the suspect was arrested one month later. Colorado authorities sought to bring Gómez García to Denver for trial, but Mexican law prohibits extradition if there is the possibility of a sentence of life without parole or the death penalty. Eventually a compromise was reached, and Gómez García was sent to the United States that December. In late 2006 he was convicted and sentenced to eighty years in prison.

On December 12, 2006, US Immigration and Customs Enforcement officials raided Swift meatpacking plants in Colorado, Texas, Iowa, Nebraska, Utah, Kentucky, and Minnesota. Their targets were immigrants who had used false documents to obtain employment. Hundreds were taken into custody, and several were summarily deported. Some decried the lack of due process and the thoughtless separation of parents from their children; others believed it was about time the government began to enforce the law.

José Antonio Gutiérrez, a Guatemalan orphaned as a child, made his way north to Los Angeles several years ago. He joined the Marines to help pay for his future university studies and as an expression of thanks to the US for giving him a chance for a different life. He was killed in Iraq on March 21, 2003, as one of the first casualties of the war. Gutiérrez was granted citizenship posthumously.[2]

Complicated Landscape

Debate over Hispanic immigration can sometimes be a heated exchange of stories, a trading of emotive accounts of untimely deaths and unjust suffering. The stories I mention are from the last decade, but they are representative of ongoing experiences. They are all too real, and therein lies their power to generate both compassion and anger. The terrible immigrant tale from Texas is one of many now in print that detail the travails of those who have braved the deserts of the Southwest, the wiles of the *coyotes*, and the watchful eyes of the border patrols. Over the past decade and a half, several thousand have perished in an effort to cross the border.[3] These experiences have been celebrated in song, such as the hit "El Mojado" ("The Wetback") by the Guatemalan singer Ricardo Arjona, the song "En mi Bolivia" by the Bolivian Yuri Ortuño and La Nueva Proyección,

2

Nicaraguan Luis Enrique's "Autobiografía," and countless ballads sung by *Norteña* bands. The accounts are as varied as anything one can imagine. That has been my own perception as I have listened to immigrants open their hearts and tell of their trek northward. But citizens of this country have also suffered violence in car wrecks, robberies, and other crimes at the hands of undocumented immigrants, some of whom have been able to evade apprehension or conviction. These victims cry out for justice, too.[4]

These sensitive stories are symptoms of a larger set of challenges related to Hispanic immigration. The multiple issues seem intractable, the number of people overwhelming. Emotions run high, and rhetoric flourishes. Metaphors used in the media heighten the perception of a massive and uncontrollable influx of foreigners. Hispanic immigration is labeled a "flood," a "rising tide" or "tidal wave," a "horde," or an "invasion." Red-flag language, such as "amnesty," the "war on terror," or the "terrible human cost" punctuates discussions that can degenerate into unfruitful diatribes. Innumerable publications, from the popular to the scholarly, and a growing number of internet sites argue their particular points of view.

In response to these differing perceptions and needs of all kinds, activist organizations—from human rights groups to border vigilantes—have sprung into action to mobilize their audiences. Selective poll data bolster a spectrum of stances, even while more circumspect polls demonstrate variations within the general population regarding such pressing issues as the possibility of providing avenues to legal work status, residency, or citizenship.[5] In the midst of all this, many Hispanics have refused to remain passive onlookers. The nation has witnessed a few mass marches in several cities, but there are also more-formal, long-standing groups that are active in lobbying local, state, and national government, working in Hispanic neighborhoods, and networking immigrant organizations.

Both political parties recognize that the Hispanic population presents the potential for millions of votes. Recent elections witnessed increased efforts by Democrats and Republicans to woo these voters and convince them that their party's commitments reflect Hispanic concerns. Some labor unions also are rallying to the immigrant cause, as they see the promise of new members to replace declining numbers. For their part, some undocumented workers visualize the unions as a means to secure better wages and protection in the workplace. The growing impact of the Hispanic electorate was especially evident in the 2012 national elections, where their vote was crucial in swing states like Florida and Colorado.[6]

Structure of the Chapter

In such a heated and convoluted atmosphere, is there any chance for thoughtful reflection? Was it always so full of twists and turns? How did we get to this point? A helpful place to begin is to take a succinct look at the history of Hispanic immigration to the United States. After this survey, I review two sets of issues that have been lightning rods: the possible effects of immigration on national identity and its impact on the economy. I add a component to each of these points that provides readers with a broader perspective on the realities "on the ground" that is rarely considered in discussions on immigration. Events and issues are often more complicated than they may seem. Perhaps the truth on these matters lies in a more nuanced middle ground, between the opposite poles of closing the border with stiff enforcement and opening it indiscriminately to all who desire to come.

I consciously avoid throwing statistics at the reader. Statistics can be impressive, but they are always disputed and can be confusing. Those who want that information will find appropriate resources in the endnotes. My focus is on how the immigration of undocumented Hispanics is described and debated in the public square. It is ideas and attitudes that I am after, not numbers.

Yet another important dimension must be addressed by those who claim to be Christians, and with this the chapter will close: How are the newly arrived Hispanics affecting the landscape of the Christian faith in the United States? How might the presence of millions of Hispanic Christians—both Catholic and Protestant—inform one's position vis-à-vis immigration? Should arguments be limited to the cultural and the economic? This chapter closes by trying to refocus the discussion on Hispanic immigration with matters of faith and ministry.

A Brief History of Hispanic Immigration

A General Orientation

Primary factors. Several theories attempt to explain the causes and process of international migration.[7] Sorting through these various perspectives lies beyond the purview of this book, but some general observations can be made with respect to the

Immigration is neither a new phenomenon nor only a recent political concern.

United States. Immigration is neither a new phenomenon nor only a recent political concern. It has been a topic of national interest since the colonial era. The internal issues, however, always have had a global backdrop.[8] That is, each major period of immigration to the United States has been part of larger migrations happening simultaneously around the world and, therefore, has been inseparable from the political, social, and economic conditions of other nations.

From the dawn of the republic, authorities have deliberated about who would be welcomed and who would be excluded. Originally, immigration was handled by the states, but the increased complications of monitoring the entrance of foreign peoples led the Supreme Court in 1875 to declare immigration to be the responsibility of the federal government. The Immigration Act of 1891 established the Office of the Superintendent of Immigration within the Treasury Department. Over the next century immigration matters were moved to the jurisdiction of the Department of Commerce and Labor (1903) and then to the Department of Labor (1913). The Immigration and Naturalization Service (INS) was created in 1933, and was located within the Department of Justice in 1940. The INS was transferred to the Department of Homeland Security in 2003, and its functions were combined with customs duties to create the Inspection and Customs Enforcement Agency (ICE). These administrative changes signal varying shifts in the perception of immigration by the government.

History demonstrates a recurring tension principally between economic concerns and different expressions of nativism. Nativism consists of feelings of fear or hatred toward a foreign minority that is believed to threaten what is assumed to be the national culture. This is not to say that the twin poles of economics and nativism define the only public responses to immigration. The outlook of the American populace as a whole usually is a combination of the two. The United States has frequently been characterized by graciousness to outsiders, and it has absorbed millions of immigrants, refugees, and asylum seekers since its founding.

The economic factors that have motivated immigration to the United States have entailed the continuous interplay between a lack of opportunities in the country of origin (the push factor) and the drive to meet the labor needs of American business, industry, and farming (the pull factor). The contrary emotions of nativism have been generated by several dynamics, depending on the particular period and circumstances: religious sentiments, ignorance or rejection of unfamiliar customs and language, racism, educational levels, and economic downturns with the attending competition for jobs. During the past 150 years the multiple conflicts between economic demands at home and abroad, popular opposition, the attitudes of organized labor, foreign policy, and the agendas of political parties have yielded a legacy of contradictory regulations and inconsistent enforcement. Confusing compromises and legal irregularities have reigned as politicians have sought to satisfy opposing constituencies.

Negative examples. Some early cases of immigrant restriction stand out. One of the most notorious was the treatment of Chinese immigrants for about a century.[9] Beginning in the late 1840s and prompted by the Gold Rush, the demands in California in agriculture, mining, and the building of the railroads fueled a search for inexpensive manpower. A solution was found in contracting workers from mainland China. Soon recruiting firms were established in Asia, and these collaborated with shipping firms to facilitate the movement of laborers to this country. The US government and Chinese authorities negotiated several trade agreements to legalize and regulate this traffic. As early as 1852, however, California locals sought to block the importation of "coolies." Brutal racial discrimination persisted for decades. "Suspicious" Chinese females were not permitted entry in order to avoid births of those of Chinese origin on US soil (and so the right to citizenship, according to the Fourteenth Amendment). All kinds of restrictions were placed on these immigrants at local levels, and violence exploded against them and their property on a number of occasions. This antipathy became national and culminated in the Chinese Exclusion Act of 1882, which in effect barred the introduction of further Chinese labor and denied the Chinese most claims to citizenship; this prohibition was renewed on several occasions. Chinese were not accorded the right to become citizens until 1943 with the passage of the Chinese Exclusion Repeal Act (the Magnuson Act). From 1910 to 1940 the official Western gateway into the US was the Angel Island Immigration Station, located in San Francisco Bay. Once the place of detention and tragic discrimination, this "Ellis Island of the West" is now a National Historic Landmark. The Senate passed a resolution in October 2011 apologizing for the discrimination that targeted the Chinese; the House passed a similar resolution in June 2012. Ironically, the decade in which the Chinese Exclusion Act was enacted also witnessed the installation of the Statue of Liberty in New York harbor, a juxtaposition that is a powerful demonstration of this country's ambivalence toward immigrants.

Another negative reaction to large-scale immigration occurred in the final quarter of the nineteenth century and the early years of the twentieth with the arrival of millions of Irish and southern Europeans, especially Italians. Opposition arose from many quarters, based on the claim that these new groups were educationally and culturally inferior, a drain on the economy, and politically problematic. Moreover, in contrast to the general Protestant flavor of the majority culture of the day, these immigrants were overwhelmingly Catholic. All of these negative features, it was felt, would damage the American ethos. A quota system to limit the admission of immigrants from certain countries was put into place with the Immigration Act of 1921 (the Quota Act) and 1924 (the Johnson-Reed Act). Another negative episode was the internment of Japanese immigrants and their descendants, many of them American citizens, in camps during the course of the Second World War.

The cruelest chapter in the history of immigration to the US, and the one with the most tragic consequences, of course, was the forced relocation here of hundreds of thousands of Africans that occurred between the seventeenth and the early nineteenth centuries. As in so many instances, this influx was prompted by labor needs. The opportunity for legal integration of these immigrants' descendants into national life would not become a possibility until the Emancipation Proclamation of 1863, and it would not become a constitutional right until the ratification of the Thirteenth Amendment in 1865 and of the Fourteenth Amendment in 1868. Nevertheless, true legal, cultural, educational, and sporting assimilation would have to await the efforts of the civil rights movement a century later. But even today, vestiges of prejudice and exclusion still remain.

Hispanic Immigration

1848–1940. Migration from Mexico and Latin America technically did not begin until 1848.[10] That was the year that the Treaty of Guadalupe-Hidalgo, which ended the Mexican-American War, was signed. With this agreement, Mexico ceded to the United States the territory that today makes up the states of California, Nevada, and Utah and parts of Arizona, New Mexico, Colorado, and Wyoming.[11] That this large swath of territory originally was part of Mexico means there has been a Hispanic presence in the United States for over a century and a half. The creation of the new national boundaries officially establishes the starting point for any immigration activity. For a number of years the land along the border of the two countries was not very populated. Several events changed that pattern between 1890 and 1929.

The prohibition against bringing in Chinese workers played a role in triggering the arrival of Mexican workers. Agriculture and industry had to look elsewhere to replace the loss of Chinese labor, and substitutes were readily at hand to the south. Ironically, the exclusion of one immigrant people opened the door to another. Another key event was the outbreak of the First World War. Hundreds of thousands of Americans joined the armed services, and the war effort created the need for even more manpower in industry. That conflict, though, halted immigration from Europe. Once again Mexican workers were available to fill the gap. To this constellation of factors can be added the political and economic situation in Mexico at that time. The agricultural and industrial decisions of President Porfirio Díaz (1876–1910) created a large landless population desperate for work, ready to move to the United States where there was a continuing demand for labor. The Mexican Revolution (1910–17) drove many more across the border in search of safety. The majority of those who came during this time span did not plan to set down permanent roots here. The goal for most was to acquire enough capital to be able to fund a new life back home. Many, of course, did stay. The US Border Patrol was founded in 1924, but its restricted presence and purpose at that time did little to stem the flow of workers from Mexico.

The situation dramatically changed toward the end of the 1920s. With the stock market crash of 1929, the onset of the Great Depression, and the desperate state of the job market, there was a backlash against foreign workers. Restrictions on immigration were added, and deportations began. Because of the difficult atmosphere, many Mexicans left of their own volition. Coincidentally, the land reform of President Lázaro Cárdenas (1934–40) made returning to Mexico an attractive option for those who desired to own property. At the same time, the problem of a lack of farm workers in California due to this exodus was resolved by the migration of the Okies to the West Coast. Once more, one people's loss proved to be another's gain.

1941–86. The next important event in US-Mexican labor relations was the 1942 signing of the *bracero* agreement (from the Spanish *brazo*, "arm"). Another world war (and a decade later the Korean War) generated the need for additional manpower and, as always, the agricultural sector was short of laborers. The *bracero* program granted visas for temporary contract work. The numbers stipulated in the treaty never satisfied the need, however, and over time undocumented immigration began to grow. In 1954, during a time of suspicion of everything foreign (the McCarthy era), the INS launched "Operation Wetback" in parts of California, Texas, and Arizona. It was designed to apprehend anyone believed to be in the country illegally. Officials claimed that over a million Latin Americans were apprehended and deported or voluntarily left the country. The *bracero* program was eventually shut down in 1965 due in large measure to pressure from unions and civil rights groups.[12]

The Immigration and Nationality Act of 1952 preserved the quota system (although the allocations were calculated differently than in the 1924 bill), set standards for labor procurement, and defined qualifications for eligibility for sponsoring family members. It was significantly impacted by new legislation in 1965 (the Hart-Cellar Immigration Bill), which reset the limits of permissible entries for any country at a maximum of 20,000. Moreover, a ceiling of 120,000 visas was imposed on the entire western hemisphere. Mexico, like every other country, was given the 20,000 allotment. This system took effect in 1968, but clearly it was utterly unrealistic in light of the history of Mexican labor in this country. An unexpected, but certainly inevitable, result was an exponential increase in undocumented immigration. The number of legal visas for Mexicans was eventually raised, but it never reached levels to match labor needs. The pressure for migration northward was exacerbated by worsening economic conditions in Mexico and the rapid increase in its population. In other words, while restrictions were growing, more and more people were trying to enter the country to find work.

In response, the Immigration Reform and Control Act (IRCA) was passed by Congress in 1986, during the Reagan administration. This was the most significant piece of legislation since 1965, and it has been the principal tool regulating issues related to immigration for the past two and a half decades. Sectors of the nation were feeling uncomfortable with the growing number of Hispanics because of the cost implications for public services and nativistic concerns. Texas, for example, passed a law excluding Hispanic children of undocumented parents from attending public schools, but this was overturned by the Supreme Court in 1982 (*Plyer v. Doe*). To control the flow of immigrants from Mexico, IRCA fortified the Border Patrol and developed more procedures and weightier sanctions for employers regarding the hiring of undocumented workers. This law also provided amnesty to those who could prove that they had been in the US since 1982 and to a special category of farm workers. In all, over three million applied for amnesty.

This new arrangement, however, did not achieve its intended outcomes. Many employers balked at the amount of required paperwork, while others simply did not want to lose their cheap source of labor. The demand for documentation spawned a black market in fraudulent papers and encouraged many employers to pay salaries in cash to evade their legal responsibilities. In addition, the preference system for reuniting families allowed those who had received amnesty to bring over their kin; this led to the admission of more people than the government had anticipated. The resulting emerging Hispanic networks and communities in turn fostered the conditions to receive and help other new immigrants. In many ways, then, IRCA proved to be counterproductive.

1986–present. Other schemes attempted to respond to these unforeseen problems. The Immigration Act of 1990 increased employer sanctions, strengthened the Border Patrol, made eligibility of family members more difficult, and sought to encourage the entry of people, especially more skilled workers, from more developed countries. The Illegal Immigration Reform and Immigrant Responsibility Act of 1996 (IIRIRA), among other things, funded increased surveillance along the border, limited access to many federal benefits for undocumented immigrants, and allowed states to reduce public services to immigrants. The Personal Responsibility and Work Opportunity Reconciliation

Act of 1996 reinforced the restrictions of IIRIRA and added others.

More recently, there have been several well-publicized attempts to pass comprehensive legislation aimed at providing solutions to the increasingly complex matter of immigration. Proposals have come from all sides of the debate, but the potentially most far-reaching did not pass both houses of Congress. For example, the Border Protection, Antiterrorism, and Illegal Immigration Control Act of 2005 (also known as the Sensenbrenner Bill) authorized the construction of seven hundred miles of fencing along the border with Mexico and added more restrictions and sanctions; it was approved by the House of Representatives but did not receive the necessary votes in the Senate. A series of compromise bipartisan bills, which attempted to wed increased border security and enforcement of sanctions with an increase in the number of visas and the provision of an avenue to residency or citizenship, have also failed: in the House, the STRIVE Act of 2007 (Security Through Regularized Immigration and a Vibrant Economy Act); in the Senate, the Secure America and Orderly Immigration Act of 2005 (the McCain-Kennedy Bill), the Comprehensive Immigration Reform Act of 2006, and the Comprehensive Immigration Reform Act of 2007 (the Secure Borders, Economic Opportunity, and Immigration Reform Act).

An initiative first introduced in the Senate in 2001 and reintroduced on several occasions, which would have provided a pathway to legal status for qualifying undocumented youth, was the DREAM (Development, Relief, and Education for Alien Minors) Act. Though it did not prosper, several states passed laws to facilitate higher education possibilities for these immigrants. In June 2012 President Barack Obama signed the DACA measure (the Deferred Action for Childhood Arrivals program). This executive order allowed certain young undocumented immigrants to apply for a renewable two-year deportation reprieve and a work permit.

This action, of course, fell short of comprehensive immigration legislation reform. As a consequence of the ramifications of the Hispanic vote in the 2012 national elections, however, significant immigration legislation could see the light of day during the 112th Congress (installed January 2013). In June of 2013 a bipartisan Senate bill on comprehensive immigration reform put forth by the "Gang of Eight" (four Democrats and four Republicans) was brought forward for debate. It sought to address the concerns of all parties in a compromise with support on both sides of the aisle. At the time of the writing of this volume, it had passed in the Senate, but its fate in the full Congress was uncertain.

During the past thirty years, as the Hispanic presence has become more prominent, a number of initiatives at local and state levels attempted to discourage immigration. These were of several kinds. Some of the more high-profile forms in three areas have been:

- Security: In 1993 Silvestre Reyes, Border Patrol chief in El Paso, Texas, organized Operation Blockade, an intense effort to intercept undocumented immigrants. It was later renamed Operation Hold the Line. Other border programs with similar purposes include: Operation Gatekeeper, San Diego, California (1994);[13] Operation Safeguard, Nogales, Arizona (1995); and Operation Rio Grande, Brownsville, Texas (1997). These strategies increased vigilance by adding patrol personnel and installing fences and floodlights, along with other defensive measures. The strictest resolution to date was Arizona Senate Bill 1070, signed into law in April 2010. This law placed heavy controls on identity, movement, and hiring practices. A few other states (like Alabama and Georgia) passed similarly stringent laws to deal with undocumented immigrants.

- Restriction of social services, health care, and public education (ballot initiatives): Proposition 187, California (1994; it was declared unconstitutional in 1998).

- English-only public education (ballot initiatives): The two most prominent at the national level were Proposition 227 in California (1998) and Proposition 200 in Arizona (2000).

Another layer of confusion and tension involves the coordination between local, state, and federal laws and agencies in relation to permissible regulations and proper jurisdiction.[14] The furor generated by Arizona Senate Bill 1070 is the most well-publicized case of these tensions. Claiming that the state had overstepped its reach, the Department of Justice challenged the bill and in federal court sought injunctions to its implementation. In June 2012 the US Supreme Court struck down several of its provisions. A few years earlier a tough law directed against undocumented Hispanic immigrants in the small Pennsylvania town of Hazleton grabbed national attention. Citing negative effects on the community's quality of life by the recent arrival of a significant number of immigrants, the city council decreed a series of fines to hinder, among other things, hiring immigrants or renting to them. A federal judge struck down the measure on July 27, 2007, claiming that setting these kinds of laws lay outside the province of local government, but the matter is still not settled.[15]

The administration of the border with Mexico has changed considerably in the wake of the attacks of September 11, 2001. The Department of Homeland Security was established in November 2002, and the INS was absorbed into the Department of Homeland Security several months later, in the spring of 2003. INS activities and the Border Patrol were folded into the newly formed Immigration and Customs Enforcement Agency (ICE), which is a bureau of the department. Border security thus became part of the more comprehensive national effort to control terrorism and drug traffic. In October 2006 President George W. Bush signed the Secure Fence Act into law. It authorized the building of a fence along the US-Mexico border along with other boosts to security personnel and technology. Along with the building of this fence, the number of Border Patrol personnel was increased.

Finally, it bears mentioning that the influx of undocumented immigrants has been dropping for the last several years, even as the number of those who return to their country of origin voluntarily has increased. There are several reasons for these recent trends. They include the lack of employment opportunities in a stagnant US economy, the increased difficulties and insecurities in everyday life generated by state and local legislation, and the greater difficulty in crossing due to the border fence and other controls. In addition, record numbers of immigrants were deported during the first term of the Obama administration.

This cursory survey of the history of immigration demonstrates the baffling and contradictory state of affairs in the United States. The path that brought the country to this point has been anything but consistent or straight. The realities concerning immigration are an unwieldy set of regulations (for the government, employers, the soliciting immigrant, and their families); huge backlogs in processing applications; an awkward synchronization between federal agencies and between these and state and local governments; prisons overcrowded with immigrants awaiting trial or deportation; more deaths due to security measures that have driven immigrants to pass through desert regions; conflicts in educational policies; an overburdened health-care system; a deeply divided public among the majority culture; and a Hispanic population that is at once hopeful, timorous, and frustrated. Any future solution will have to be as intricately complex as the many facets of the present situation. No legislation can satisfy everyone, nor will it be without its own inherent problems. To unravel the muddle is a tall order and will be messy business. That is the only thing that is certain.

As the country tries to move forward (even if new legislation were to be passed), two central issues continually come to the fore: the question of national identity and the potential economic impact of Hispanic immigration. I will deal with each one of these topics in turn and introduce additional components to each about which readers may be unaware.

Who Are "We"? The Question of National Identity

The Threat to "Americanness"

Demographics.[16] The official government census states that in 2010 there were 50.5 million Hispanics in the United States (the inclusion of Puerto Rico would add 3.7 million to that number),[17] a figure that represented 16 percent of the total population.

What will "American" mean in twenty years? Will it even be a relevant term?

These statistics reveal that between 2000 and 2010 the Hispanic population increased by 43 percent and accounted for over half of the growth of the country's total population. This rapid increase was due to immigration and a comparatively higher birthrate.[18] Estimates on how many Hispanics are undocumented range from eleven million to twelve million, the largest group being of Mexican origin. It is hard to know what percentage of this demographic is represented in the census data, as many were fearful of being counted and perhaps exposing themselves to potential apprehension and deportation by ICE. Though historically Hispanics migrated primarily to the Southwest (especially to California and Texas), their presence today is truly a national phenomenon. Hispanics have supplanted African Americans as the largest minority group in the country.

What worries many are the possible changes in national character that might result from this significant demographic shift. How might this large influx change the cultural landscape? What will "American" mean in twenty years? Will it even be a relevant term? Will English still be the dominant language? Samuel Huntington, author of the best seller *The Clash of Civilizations*, sounds an alarm in a more recent book, *Who Are We?*[19] Slowly but surely, he claims, the markers of classic American identity are being buried by millions of new immigrants, especially those from Latin America.

The treasured cultural core includes what Huntington calls America's historic "creed" of liberal democracy, individualism, private property, and the market. These are all important commitments for the people of the United States, but this creed is not ultimately what makes this country unique. The heart of the national identity, he says, is its Anglo-Protestant beliefs and values, the English language, and the legacy of Western European culture.

Cultural assimilation. Huntington claims that, unlike earlier immigrants, new arrivals today are not assimilating at the same rate or with the same conviction to leave behind their original national identity. In fact, they seem reluctant to do so, and several factors work against their assimilation. The immigration from Latin America is different from previous periods in several ways. To begin with, the Mexican border is contiguous with the United States. The home country is not an ocean away, as it was for those coming from Europe or Asia a century ago. Entry and movement back and forth between north and south are much easier, so fewer feel the need to adapt to the mores and language of the host country. In addition, the sheer quantity of Hispanic immigrants dwarfs anything in history. They are also persistent. Neither failure to make it past border patrols nor deportation back to their countries of origin are sufficient deterrents to discourage them from trying again and again.

Third, these immigrants tend to concentrate in certain parts of the country and live within enclaves in those areas, thereby slowing down their integration into the larger society.

Evidence of this lack of assimilation, according to Huntington, is found in declining levels of English language acquisition, less educational achievement, and poorer socioeconomic success. There also is a lack of enthusiasm, he says, to seek American citizenship in comparison with immigrant groups from other parts of the world. Hispanics appear to want to maintain their language, their customs, and even their foreign citizenship, even as they take advantage of the new way of life afforded by their work here. The disinclination to accept this country's historical culture and to forswear their national allegiances, Huntington argues, is abetted by certain sectors of academia, the media, and political elites as part of a defense of multiculturalism. The efforts of these groups seriously compound the problem of the slow pace or even the possibility of assimilation.

Other prominent figures echo Huntington's concerns and agree with his negative assessment of multiculturalism and its role in impeding the assimilation process.[20] Mark Krikorian adds that the internet and inexpensive phone access also hinder assimilation and expresses worry over the increase in the immigrant population. Victor Davis Hanson relates how his home state of California has changed in the past two decades, sliding toward becoming what he creatively labels "Mexifornia." In his view, legislators, educators, and other activists have fostered an attitude of victimization among Hispanics and have sanctioned the separation of races—a new form of tribalism—all of which makes the governance of the state more difficult and has brought California to the brink of financial disaster. The very things about this country that would have drawn Mexicans and other Latin Americans here in the first place, such as participation in a vibrant economy and educational achievement with all of the horizons it can open, are being cordoned off. The result, Hanson says, is that the life immigrants lead often becomes a sad cycle of despair in which they navigate the dark underside of illegality. Of course, businesspeople, who continue to offer jobs to immigrants and pay little, perpetuate the quagmire.

Former Colorado Congressman Tom Tancredo and syndicated columnist and news-show pundit Pat Buchanan are more shrill in their tone.[21] The titles of their books, *In Mortal Danger* and *State of Emergency*, respectively, veritably shout gloom and doom. Like Hanson, these authors underscore the damaging impact on public services and education and decry bilingualism. They emphasize, too, the activities of brutal Hispanic gangs (in particular the Mara Salvatrucha or M-13) and the escalation of drug trafficking along the border. Tancredo connects Hispanic immigration to concerns for post-9/11 security and claims that terrorists ("Islamofascists") are slipping through the porous boundary with Mexico. Buchanan goes so far as to argue that a concerted *reconquista* (the retaking by peaceful means of what formerly was part of Mexico) is under way, masterminded by Mexican government officials and elites.

Hispanic voices. Some high profile Hispanics have presented their lives, at least to some degree, as testimonies to significant assimilation to the majority culture, in particular with respect to the learning of English and the ideal of educational advancement. One of the better known is the former director of the US Commission on Civil Rights, neoconservative Linda Chávez. Another, but from a very different ideological perspective, is the editorialist Richard Rodríguez. Both believe ethnic issues should be dealt with in the private realm because in the public sector they are more likely to take the form of sociopolitical constructs than reflect reality. Yet in neither case has the road been uncomplicated or without personal cost. Chávez has been sharply criticized by certain Hispanic activists and others for her assimilationist opinions on such matters; at the same time, she has been viciously attacked for stating that she believes that racism lies behind some of the anti-immigrant feelings in this country.[22] Rodríguez is dismissive of what he characterizes as tangled thinking regarding the notion of "Hispanic," yet he has written an eloquent trilogy that traces the difficult path he traveled to arrive at his own stance.[23]

Hispanics and the Identity Predicament

Are these worries about the possible harm to national identity legitimate? Are they a fair appraisal of the cultural landscape? Can more restrictive measures preserve "Americanness"? On the one hand, increased controls on undocumented immigrants serve to isolate that group in many ways. Ironically, then, they keep these Hispanics from incorporating themselves fully into national life, or at the very least slow that process down. They help ensure that the identity complaint becomes a self-fulfilling prophecy. On the other hand, careful reflection from a broader point of reference reveals that issues surrounding identity are more multifaceted than simply the majority culture's anxiety over the loss of what it considers to be its central values and way of life.

Hispanics elsewhere. To begin with, unease about a surge in Hispanic immigration is not limited to the United States. In recent years Hispanics have also been migrating to Europe. As is the case in this country, issues related to *coyotes* and immigrant safety and rights, potential economic effects, and national identity are the discussion points in public discourse and political planning.[24] In a paradoxical reversal of history, the nations of Europe that in the past experienced the emigration of millions of their own to other places are today a destination for immigrants.

The movement from Latin America has been going on for some time, and tougher legal restrictions and greater difficulties for entering into the US have increased migration across the Atlantic Ocean. Spain is a case in point. It is a remarkable case, too, because there are many commonalities between that

"Mother Country" and the Spanish-speaking nations that historically were its colonies. In Spain, even while low birth rates and the economy in fact require the absorption of a large number of newcomers, racial tensions are rising and new restrictive laws are being put into place.[25] The cultural fears felt in the United States, then, are natural emotions for any host country. They also fit into the nativistic patterns, mentioned earlier, that have recurred throughout US history. But is the concern for identity limited to the majority culture? Should the discussion of cultural identity be reconfigured and expanded?

Hispanic identity. Clearly, Hispanics in the United States wrestle with identity too. They are struggling with who they are and what they might become in the inescapable processes of cultural adaptation. Like most immigrants, Hispanics have to become acquainted with and live in unfamiliar settings while removed from their social and kinship networks and support. They wonder how they are to raise their children with the positive values of Latin American culture that sometimes clash with those of North American consumerism and individualism. Love of their home country and culture pulls at their heart strings. There are also the contradictory emotions over the well-being of family members left behind and the pressure to send money back to help, even as immigrants strive to make a go of life here.

For many younger Hispanics arriving today and those of the second and third generation, however, the primary issue is no longer learning how to navigate a strange system to find work. Allegiance to the country and culture of their parents is not the same. The challenge is deeper and focused elsewhere. The United States is now more home than a target destination; it is not just the land of opportunity for a better-paying job. Every dimension of life as a minority must be negotiated with the world that surrounds them: skin color, the language of the home and the language of the public sphere, accents, slang, music, religion, social status, cultural rituals (like the *quinceañera*), food, sports, and fashion styles. The crucial point is that the very fact that this give-and-take is happening is ample proof that *assimilation is taking place*.[26]

This complicated set of changes and redefinitions has become the focus of multiple sociological and anthropological studies that probe how immigrants live their lives "over here" and what "back there" comes to mean over time. Some of the titles are captivating (*From Cuenca to Queens* by Ann Miles and *New Destination Dreaming* by Helen Marrow), others revealing (*Mexican New York* by Robert Courtney Smith). This research reveals that multiple factors, such as modern technology, economic globalization, and the mobility of people, are producing cultural and linguistic hybrids and multiple loyalties that are part of a phenomenon called "transnationalism," a new field of research along with "diaspora" studies.[27] In other words, the acquisition of English and other assimilation benchmarks that the majority culture might have are not straightforward bullet points on a checklist. Hispanics are learning the language at a steady pace and adapting in many ways, but there is a whole constellation of processes occurring simultaneously in the home (the home in the US and the home in the native country), workplace, church, school, and shopping mall.[28]

The pain of becoming and understanding a different identity mix is a constant theme of Hispanic literature. Works by novelists who have roots in both North America and south of the border, such as Francisco Goldman (Guatemala), Sandra Cisneros and Victor Villaseñor (Mexico), Edmundo Paz Soldán (Bolivia), and Julia Álvarez (Dominican Republic), depict the conflicts of heart and mind of the immigrant or descendant vis-à-vis their Latin American heritage and their life in the United States. With a beauty and an intricacy worthy of their topic, these writers explore the strain felt in being somewhere and nowhere at the same time, in feeling the struggle between the memories and traces of before and the realities of the moment, in living in that in-between place within their adopted country and with ties to their homeland—all of this very difficult to articulate, but so authentic, so agonizing to the soul.[29]

Cisneros closes her magnificent work *Caramelo or Puro Cuento* with a lament of her main character, Celaya ("Lala") Reyes. Lala has come to the realization that she cannot integrate easily into Mexico City, but neither can she fit neatly into San Antonio or Chicago. At this point in her life the multiple pieces of culture, family, and country that reside deep within her are too hard to reconcile into a coherent whole:

> And I don't know how it is with anyone else, but for me these things, that song, that time, that place, are all bound together in a country I am homesick for, that doesn't exist anymore. They never existed. A country I invented. Like all emigrants caught between here and there.[30]

There is angst, but there is also the sense of growing into another kind of person—although that is not yet defined for her at the moment. Living "in the hyphen" (Mexican-American, Cuban-American, etc.) is a pilgrimage of joy and sadness, of frustration and self-discovery, of appreciation for the past and anticipation of the future, a life of hybridity.

The reaction of other Hispanics to this dilemma, in contrast, has been to celebrate the fact of difference. The initial coming together of races and cultures in what is now Latin America occurred centuries ago, when the Spanish came to the New World and conquered the indigenous peoples. That first blending of blood, symbolized forever in Latin American lore in the relationship between the *conquistador* Hernán Cortés and the Aztec woman Malintzín ("La Malinche"), produced the first *mestizos* (those of mixed race). Later would come the amalgamation with Africans (most of whom were brought over as slaves) in the Caribbean and along the Atlantic coastline, and with European settlers. Hispanics are the heirs of this grand *mestizaje* (mixture) in all of its richness and variety.[31] There is great worth in this legacy that many simply are not aware of. Some activists use this distinctive heterogeneous identity as a rallying cry against any degradation they feel victimizes Hispanics; *mestizaje* allows them to stand up to the majority culture with pride. Such a reaction is not surprising, but another constructive means of appreciating this concept is possible.

The inevitable convergence of this Hispanic diversity and the majority culture can be interpreted as yet another chapter in the ongoing historical process of *mestizaje*. New combinations are being born of both cultures, as each mutually enriches and ener-

The United States is in the midst of a transition time, and that inexorable renovation is unavoidably awkward and often painful—for all parties.

gizes the other. The result will be unexpected variations for the common good. Each cultural mix brings unique gifts (and weaknesses, too), but in the end the metamorphosis will benefit all.[32] This is not romantic optimism. I am aware of the many difficulties and the great discomfort inherent in this transformation, but I am also convinced that change is certain and that it will be fruitful.

The future of national identity. Whither identity or, perhaps better, identities? The United States is in the midst of a transition time, and that inexorable renovation is unavoidably awkward and often painful—for all parties. But then again American identity has never been a static entity. It has meant different things at diverse times, as millions from all over the world have come to this country and have added their part. African Americans were forcefully kept from the cultural mainstream for the longest time, first as slaves and later as a despised minority. The Civil War and civil rights legislation were not enough to guarantee that those Americans could become part of, let alone participate in defining, the national identity. That singular process is still ongoing and uneven. With Hispanic immigration, as with other groups, American life is being reshaped again.

The metaphor of the "melting pot" is an idea that is regularly bantered about in discussions about assimilation. A flaw in the metaphor, as commonly understood, is that it can convey the notion that, as new elements are brought in, things essentially remain the same. Besides the tricky problem of determining who should define what the "same" is and what its boundaries are, there are at least two mistaken ideas of this conception of the melting-pot model. First, history contradicts the belief that there is some fixed cultural and linguistic core that has endured unchanged over long periods of time. The facts say otherwise. Second, the adaptation process for host country or immigrant is never easy or neutral, precisely because it is not a natural turning back to or a conversion to some pristine essence. It is a melding together of a minority into and within the majority culture, but the end product is unpredictable and open ended. It has always been so. These developments are an opportunity for an enhancement of national identity, not a threat to be warded off at all costs.[33]

Economic Realities: What Does Hispanic Immigration Cost?

In addition to the arguments over cultural impact, discussions also revolve around the economics of immigration. That is, disagreements arise over the actual and potential costs and benefits of Hispanic immigration. Do local, state, and federal tax revenues generated by immigrants outweigh the amount of money required for their health care, education, law enforcement, and welfare? Should the money gathered from taxes be the sole indicator of revenue? Is it enough to consider economic issues only from the perspective of what is happening within the United States, or are they part of global economic realities?

The Impact on Jobs and Public Services

Basic complaints. Tom Tancredo presents in popular fashion four of the economic arguments commonly used to promote a more restrictive immigration policy.[34] He contends, to begin with, that the children of undocumented immigrants are an added financial burden on local school systems. New programs must be crafted to meet their special needs, such as English as a Second Language. This, in turn, requires hiring more teachers and translates into greater expense for additional classrooms, supplies, and utilities. Increased numbers also create the necessity of providing extra meals and transportation. Second, among these immigrants are many criminals, and the cost of their incarceration is crippling the prison system. Third, the fact that immigrants are willing to accept below-average wages drives down the income of American citizens. As the market adjusts to this lower pay scale, legal workers are forced to accept less than their proper due. Last, Tancredo contends, health care is being adversely affected by the presence of undocumented immigrants. Hospitals legally cannot turn away patients from emergency services, even if they cannot pay for treatment. Hospitals and ultimately state governments have to absorb the unpaid expenses. As a result, emergency rooms around the country are closing down because they are no longer financially viable.

To these four points could be added others. Among them is the contention that the revenue gained from sales tax on the purchases made by undocumented Hispanics, the property taxes on their residences, and the Social Security contributions and state and federal taxes paid by a certain percentage of these immigrants do not offset the costs listed in the preceding paragraph. Another is that the billions of dollars sent as remittances to the families of immigrants (both legal and undocumented) in Latin America are a net loss to the US economy.[35]

The restrictive policy position has its popularizers, but it also has sophisticated advocates. Think tanks and organizations such as the Center for Immigration Studies, the Federation for American Immigration Reform (FAIR), and the Heritage Foundation conduct research on immigration and then make this information available on their websites.[36] For those who desire to delve deeper, there are more scholarly publications written by experts or based on academic conferences. These tend to present a more nuanced overview of the present situation than sometimes is available in material geared to a broader audience.

One example would be the issue of the cost of social services.[37] Several variables need to be understood to fully grasp the present state of affairs. First, it is important to be aware that local, state, and federal governments have different sets of expenditures, depending on the programs used by immigrants. In addition, the cost to state governments varies according to the number and kinds of programs available to the immigrant and the generosity of their benefits. Other fundamental variables include the size of the immigration population relative to the general population and the kinds of tax revenues that are collected (for instance, is there a state income tax?). These factors differ state by state, so the fiscal effects of the utilization of services by immigrants fluctuate across the country.

Policy alternatives. Proposed policy options of those seeking rigorous immigration controls (I am avoiding the views of the reactionary fringe) that might respond to the financial challenges are directed at both internal and external realities. Internal measures would involve, for instance, placing more pressure on employers not to hire undocumented immigrants. Some state and local laws are stringent by design in order that these immigrants will self-deport or at least leave these areas. External measures include regulating the flow of people across the border. This is accomplished by physical means (the wall along the border, more patrols and technology, etc.) and by developing different admission policies that would define types of immigrants and how many in each category could be admitted. One proposal is to make entry skill based, targeting the better educated and more highly trained instead of leaving the door open to the poor and less academically qualified.[38] The idea is that competent folk could stimulate business and innovation and would contribute more in taxes because they would receive a higher income; these individuals are also likely to employ fewer public services and would be able to pay for any they might use. Another option is to gear the number of entry permits (both long-term and temporary) to the specific annual needs of agricultural, manufacturing, and service industries. This figure would change year by year, and immigrant quotas would adjust accordingly.

Immigration and the Global Economy

Alternative research. Those who argue for policies more favorable to the undocumented immigrant dispute the data and analyses of those of the restrictive persuasion.[39] They respond to each of the points raised above. For instance, a more open position emphasizes that the economic impact of undocumented immigrants cannot be limited to tax revenues and service costs. Taking into account the billions of dollars of Hispanic consumer spending and the many different kinds of industries sustained by Hispanic labor yields a very different economic evaluation, one that supports the notion that Hispanic immigration actually contributes to the national well-being. What is more, the rate of incarceration for criminal activities is much lower among Hispanics than the general population. All social groups of any size have a percentage that will be criminal; this is unavoidable and expected. The fact that the percentage is significantly less than among those who are native-born should discourage unfair stereotyping of immigrants.

Other important issues are also brought to the table. I cite only two. One is that to sustain the Social Security system there is a pressing need for a huge influx of taxable workers. Demographic projections of the aging native population indicate that the system cannot continue much longer without a large new revenue source. This need is one argument for the legalization of undocumented immigrants so that all these workers, without exception, pay into the system. Second, employment studies point out that some of the fastest growing occupational categories will be in the service industry, which employs sizeable numbers of unskilled labor in jobs that do not require a high level of education. Not only is the native-born labor force getting older, it is also becoming more educated. On both counts it cannot meet the nation's future labor requirements in these job sectors, but this is precisely the niche that many immigrants can and do fill.

I mention these counterpoints without further detail. They are crucial for a more informed point of view that can respond to the overly negative perceptions of Hispanic immigration. It is enough for my purposes, though, to make readers aware of several of these points of contention in the economic debate. My intent, as in the case of national identity, is to direct attention elsewhere, beyond the usual boundaries of discussion.

It is natural to focus attention on the multiple economic effects immigration has on the host country, in this case the United States. But also to be considered is its impact on the sending, or home, country. What is more, remittances (the movement of capital) and immigration (the movement of labor) are components of the modern global economy.

Remittances. Let us begin with the issue of remittances. In 2011 Guatemala received $4.4 billion in remittances.[40] On the positive side of the ledger, with this money families can improve their housing situation and their general economic status. With the increased cash, there is more consumer spending, which helps the local and national economy in many ways. The impact is evident not only in metropolitan areas, but also in the countryside. One can see the difference these funds have made, for instance, in the highlands. It is not difficult to guess which families have members in the US. Their houses are now made of concrete block, not adobe. They often will have a second story and a small store at street level. The money, in other words, has been invested in improvements and used to start a small business. Many immigrants not only help their families, they also contribute to community projects such as roads and park maintenance in their villages and towns. In fact, one of the topics of discussion in international development is how governments might be able to direct a certain portion of these funds for community improvement. El Salvador already has a matching funds program in place to encourage contributions from expatriates.

But there also is a negative aspect to the millions of dollars pouring into Guatemala. The quantity fluctuates according to changes in the US and global economies, such as the construction industry, and according to the political climate. When anti-immigrant sentiment is high, the flow of remittances drops.

The Guatemalan government is also aware that over time remittances inevitably will decrease. It is now working to create other job opportunities at home and find other sources of outside revenue (increased tourism, foreign investments, etc.). In addition, the loss of labor to the US has lowered agriculture and industry indicators, and in some cases the incentive to work has been adversely affected. (If it is possible to receive more in remittances than what can be earned in the fields and factories, why work?) The presence of hard currency has made prices rise and the cost of land go up; it has also maintained the exchange rate of the national currency, the *quetzal*, at an unrealistic level.

The trek north of the father and/or sons sometimes puts acute pressure on the family members left behind (wives, grandparents, children) to meet daily needs without the presence of wage-earning males. For those whose move has not gone well, the loans taken out or the properties mortgaged to pay the *coyote* and other expenses now become a terrible financial burden to the family in Guatemala.

The remittances, in other words, are both blessing and bane. The point is that the economics of Hispanic immigration has wider implications than just what occurs within the United States. For good or ill, *all* of the Americas—North, Central, and South—are invested in the remittances. We need to move beyond the simplistic rhetoric of much of the national debate. Whatever policy is chosen will affect the economies and social well-being of the entire hemisphere. And if things go badly in Latin America, the ripple effect back to the US would be disastrous. This is a reality one must accept in a global economy.

Global migrant labor. At an even broader level, the migration of labor is a worldwide phenomenon that is impacting sending and receiving countries on every continent. Many millions are on the move seeking work and a new life. International economic agreements now must come to grips with the inescapable effect of globalization. This was an unforeseen consequence in some cases and is now becoming a discussion point in newer developments.[41]

One illustration of this is the North American Free Trade Agreement (NAFTA) between the US, Canada, and Mexico, which was launched in 1994. NAFTA's principal purpose was to free up the flow of capital, manufactured goods, and services among these countries. What has become increasingly obvious is that it is not realistic to expect goods and services to move freely (with the lowering of production costs and consumer prices as one of the expectations) and not anticipate labor to move across borders as well. The loss of manufacturing jobs in the US due to the transfer of production to other countries has fueled internal migration by native-born workers in search of new employment and a better life. The same is happening in Latin America. In the case of Mexico, the impact of NAFTA has been mixed. There have been massive job losses, especially in the agricultural sector, and the country is losing ground in the manufacturing battle with other countries, such as China. Mexican labor, therefore, has journeyed northward. This is a human response, and it is worldwide.[42]

The migration of labor—of skilled and unskilled, temporary and more permanent workers—has been an important topic in other international negotiations. The General Agreement on Trade in Services (a treaty of the World Trade Organization—WTO) and the Doha Developmental Round of negotiations of 2001–8 (which was sponsored by the WTO) both include the movement of labor as an agenda item. The Doha Round, whatever its shortcomings, had been organized to design agreements that ideally would benefit primarily developing countries. Its advocates viewed these talks as an expression of the moral obligation of more powerful nations to help move the entire world forward toward greater economic growth and social stability. The economic challenges related to labor were one dimension of this duty.

These larger economic realities show that, while the present debate must deal with the close-at-hand impact of Hispanic immigration, it will not do to leave the discussion at a purely national level. A much wider set of dynamics is at work that needs to be recognized and factored in. The United States is part of a world economy. The workings of global capitalism are affecting financial realities here and abroad in multiple ways, good and bad, and they are all interconnected. The migration of labor is part of this tapestry. And this is a very large piece of cloth indeed, one that is infinitely complex.

The Ignored Dimension: Christian Faith and Hispanics

Hopefully, it is now evident that the historical, cultural, and economic topics that fuel so much rhetoric in this country are much more intricate than many suppose. The backdrop for a more informed discussion will consider the long trajectory of how we got to where we are today and will include an appreciation of the very broad cultural and economic realities that make up Hispanic immigration.

There is still another facet of life that needs to be mentioned, and it can lead to an even fuller understanding of the current scene. This dimension is religion—more specifically, the Christian faith. This important piece of Hispanic identity rarely appears in the national debate. This omission is odd because all who know something of the history and culture of Latin America are well aware that it is overwhelmingly religious. Most Hispanics arrive in the United States with some type of Christian background and awareness.

The New Pulse in Christian Churches

Hispanic Christianity. Christian faith is vibrant among the immigrant population.[43] The first and most obvious indication of the presence of Hispanic Christians is the increase in the numbers of attendees in churches on a Sunday morning. The face of North American Catholicism is changing, and the church is growing. Masses in parishes around the country are burgeoning with recent arrivals from south of the border (a little more than two-thirds of first-generation Hispanic immigrants are Catholic). Estimates place the number of Hispanic Protestant congregations of all stripes in the United States in the many thousands. Mainline denominations, but especially evangelical and Pentecostal denominations and independent groups, are seeing new churches sprout up everywhere. These congregations meet in basements and fellowship halls of existing Anglo churches, in storefronts, and in homes; some have acquired their own facilities. Church size ranges from small assemblies of a few dozen worshipers to those where thousands gather. Associations of pastors and leaders are being organized, of which the most prominent among evangelicals are the National Hispanic Christian Leadership Conference, Esperanza, and the National Latino Evangelical Coalition. The National Hispanic Prayer Breakfast, a fruit of Esperanza's efforts, is now an annual event in Washington, DC. The nation is taking notice of this growing Hispanic religious presence too. The cover of the April 15, 2013, edition of *Time* read "The Latino Revolution."

The landscape of Hispanic Christianity is as diverse as Hispanic culture, and this variety makes any sort of simplistic generalizations impossible. Some features, though, are worth pointing

Christian faith is vibrant among the immigrant population, which now numbers in the millions.

out. For instance, Hispanic Catholicism is influenced by the popular (sometimes syncretistic), communal, and celebratory faith of the Americas.[44] The Virgin of Guadalupe and the saints are much more important than in Anglo-Catholicism. Easter week processions, *posadas* at Christmas time, and other traditional observances are beginning to appear. Interestingly, over half of Hispanic Catholics classify themselves as charismatic.

In many places Pentecostals make up the majority of Protestant Hispanic churches and usually have the largest congregations.[45] Some of these churches belong to historic Pentecostal denominations, such as the Assemblies of God and the Church of God, Cleveland. Others are mission churches planted by Latin

American neo-Pentecostal denominations. In metro Denver I know of several groups whose mother churches are in Guatemala: Iglesia Elim, El Shaddai, and Palabra en Acción. There also are those that began here in the US and do not have formal connections with any organization. These Pentecostal and neo-Pentecostal churches have their own particular flavor: exuberance and joy in worship, a reverence for the Bible, a strong commitment to evangelism, an interest in the last days, and in some cases the celebration of a gospel of prosperity and healing. In addition, some Hispanic denominational churches manifest configurations that are different from their majority-culture counterparts. One can find Baptists with a more vibrant tone, and congregations of mainline churches might have Pentecostal touches and an interest in evangelism and Bible study that normally are associated with evangelicalism.

In addition to functioning as sanctuaries for worship, Hispanic churches serve as networking centers for finding jobs and helping those in need; some work to connect immigrants to appropriate resources for getting their legal matters straightened out. Congregations may also take on the role of the extended family of Latin American culture. It is not uncommon to see Hispanic churches meeting together in a park on a Sunday afternoon, sharing the meal and warmth that would have been reserved for Sunday gatherings at a relative's house in their "former life." In some instances in the past, and increasingly more in the present, churches have mobilized for social and political causes.[46]

Hispanic ministries. The Catholic Church and many Protestant denominations see this explosion in the number of churches and churchgoers as an unprecedented opportunity for all kinds of pastoral and caring ministries. It has also led to the establishment of training institutions all over the country. The Catholic Church, Protestant denominations, and several seminaries have begun programs at different educational levels to help meet the need for equipped laity and pastors for this burgeoning Christian body. In the past two decades the number of Hispanic persons with graduate degrees has been on the rise. There are now professional organizations for Hispanic theologians, such as ACHTUS (Academy of Catholic Hispanic Theologians of the United States) and AETH (Asociación para la Educación Teológica Hispana), and several academic theological journals. English-speaking publishing houses of a breadth of persuasions have begun to publish works in English by these theologians or have incorporated a Spanish wing (sometimes by acquiring Latin American publishers). One also could mention the proliferation of recording labels for gospel singers of all styles of music, glossy magazines with different target audiences, youth conventions and rallies, and seminars for pastors and laypeople focusing on a wide variety of topics of interest.

All of these are elements of a fast-growing Christian Hispanic culture that is as multifaceted and diverse in its beliefs and activities as that of the majority Christian culture—albeit with its own distinctive flavor. This phenomenon is not just something to be aware of or to be considered simply a new target for outreach; it contains perspectives that have much to teach majority-culture Christians and their churches about life with God. Both Christian cultures have much to learn from each other and should begin to reflect on how to work together for the kingdom of God. Interestingly, within many Hispanic congregations one also witnesses the impact of the dynamics of immigrant assimilation, such as the shift in language preference from Spanish to English between first- and second-generation immigrants and their youth. In many cases high school- and college-age Hispanic Christians gravitate to the youth groups of Anglo churches because of the language, music, and more attractive activities that are possible because of the higher economic status of these Anglo congregations. Hispanic ministry is exceedingly complex, lively, and full of amazing potential.[47]

In speaking of Hispanic immigration, therefore, one must be aware that with this movement of millions have come countless believers and that many others are coming to faith after they arrive in the United States. For the Christian, Hispanic immigration can no longer be conceived as an anonymous mass of people or reduced to arguments over statistics. Many immigrants are brothers and sisters in Christ, who deserve all the respect and attention this fact should engender in those of the majority culture who claim to love and follow Jesus.

The "Browning" of Christianity

This spiritual and ecclesiological appreciation of Hispanic immigration can be broadened still further by placing it within the context of changes in the profile of Christianity at the global level. During the past one hundred years, Roman Catholicism and Protestantism of all stripes have experienced explosive growth in Africa, Asia, and Latin America. The greater part of Christians now live outside North America and Western Europe. Some characterize this movement of Christianity's center of gravity as the "browning" or "globalizing" of the faith.

Philip Jenkins is one who has charted this population shift and its increasing effect on the face of Christianity. In his book *The Next Christendom*, now in its third edition, he describes the vibrant energy of groups from the Southern Hemisphere, or global South.[48] Jenkins highlights their belief in the supernatural and healing, fresh worship styles, concern for social justice, and robust commitment to evangelism. This especially typifies evangelical and Pentecostal churches, which are the fastest-growing groups. Another trait Jenkins focuses on, which he has developed more fully in a newer work, is a strong adherence to the Bible.[49] These believers are overwhelmingly a people of the Book, people who cherish the Scriptures. What often distinguishes them on a Sunday morning is that they carry a Bible under their arm.

They gladly memorize passages, devote themselves to biblical study, and try to apply its teachings to all areas of life with the profound conviction of its immediacy and relevance. Of course, these very same characteristics also pertain to many Hispanic churches in the United States, whose members are part of this global phenomenon.

Still another feature of this incarnation of the Christian faith is its missionary spirit. The global South has become a launching pad for a fresh missionary movement, with countries such as Nigeria and South Korea leading the way in commissioning missionaries and establishing missionary training centers and agencies. From its inception, Christianity has been a mobile faith, always on the move, always sending out messengers of the Word into new areas and planting churches on virgin soil. As a result, the demographic, administrative, and educational hub of the Christian faith has shifted progressively over time from the eastern Mediterranean to Europe to the United States, and now to several locations in the South. In the past few decades, and still more in the years to come, Berlin, London, New York City, Chicago, Wheaton, Colorado Springs, and Los Angeles have given way to Nairobi, Seoul, São Paulo, Guatemala City, and other metropolises in the Two-Thirds or Majority World.[50]

What does this seismic shift in Christianity have to do with Hispanic immigration? The answer lies in appreciating the breadth and power of what God is doing in the world today. The zeal of this "next Christendom" finds expression in the many organized efforts on the part of institutions in the South to propagate the faith around the world. At the same time, the spread of this fresh wave of Christianity is occurring by means of the migration of millions of believers, who now are impacting their new lands. In fact, "diaspora missiology" is a growing field of research and ministry. Missiologists from around the world are trying to better understand these displaced groups and reflect on how to mobilize the Christians among them to accomplish the mission of God.[51]

From this perspective, could what we are witnessing in this country be part of a new, divinely directed global phenomenon? Is God bringing millions of Hispanics to the United States to revitalize the Christian churches here and to present to those who do not yet believe the opportunity to turn to Christ in their search for a new life? Many Hispanics and pastors sincerely believe that God has led them here for a purpose: to play an important role in a revival of the Christian faith in this country.

In other words, if Christians of the majority culture take a very different look at Hispanic immigration, they will see that something much bigger than they might have imagined is happening. The church of Jesus Christ is growing and being impacted in unexpected ways. This work of God is part of an enormous movement that spans the globe.

Conclusion

In the introduction I stated that the title *Christians at the Border* has a literal and a metaphorical dimension. This chapter has offered a long reflection on the literal dividing line between the United States and Mexico that runs from the Gulf of Mexico to the Pacific Ocean. We have looked at the history of Hispanic immigration and then probed two of the most hotly contested topics: national identity and economic impact. In each case my goal has been to demonstrate just how complicated these issues are. They are unbelievably multifaceted. The last section added still another piece to the complex puzzle: the presence of millions of Hispanic Christians.

Many now are becoming interested in the topic of immigration for the first time and are getting involved with immigrants. In fact, over the last few years among Christians of all persuasions there has been a significant shift in perspective toward immigrants, whether documented or undocumented. On the one hand, national associations and denominations from across the theological spectrum have made statements advocating a positive attitude toward immigrants and supporting ministry to them. A list of declarations appears in the appendix. At the same time, both mainline and evangelical groups have launched major advocacy initiatives. The National Council of Churches through Church World Service and many member churches are involved in a variety of efforts at many levels. The National Association of Evangelicals released a resolution on immigration in 2009, and World Relief, its humanitarian arm, created the *Welcoming the Stranger* curriculum and has organized conferences on several college campuses. It also has teamed with the Evangelical Free Church's Immigrant Hope ministry to develop the Immigrant Pathway Institute, which trains attendees in immigration law to facilitate their earning Board of Immigration Appeals certification to legally function as non-attorneys in immigration cases. A major event was the establishment of the Evangelical Immigration Table (EIT) in June 2012. EIT has signatories representing a broad range of constituencies and has funded local, state, and national programs to engage immigration issues with churches and leaders.

What is more, immigration is bringing together all kinds of Christians to work shoulder to shoulder for change. While theological and ideological differences remain on other topics, there is a healthy consensus on immigration. We are witnessing occasional cooperation between groups that often have viewed each other with suspicion.

Where are we to ground our convictions on immigration and this new enthusiasm? For many of us, the ultimate source for this wisdom is the Bible. It is not uncommon, though, for Christians to know nothing of what the Bible might have to contribute to the topic; others have sympathy toward immigrants born of a general sense of Christian charity but not informed by Scripture. For both tendencies, orientation is needed. For that reason, the next three chapters will examine how the divine Word might shed light on the national debate. This will be the next border to cross. Accounts in the Bible of the migration of people are pervasive, and there is a constant emphasis on displaying appropriate attitudes to the outsider. The amount of biblical material relevant to immigration issues today may prove to be surprising.

The contention of this book is this: if Christians want to address the problems posed by the immigration of Hispanic peoples and contribute to possible solutions, then they should do so consciously *as Christians* and more specifically *as biblically informed Christians.*

2

Of Immigrants, Refugees, and Exiles

Guidance from the Old Testament, Part I

I have poor eyesight. For many, many years I wore bifocals. I cannot see either close up or far away without help. The computer age complicated my situation. For a while I had a separate pair of eyeglasses for working with my laptop, because the screen sits in that intermediate space that neither part of the bifocal could handle well. Now I have progressive lenses. What is worse, if I want to read the small print on a label, I have to take off my glasses altogether and bring the writing up close to make out the words! Without my glasses I can still see—even if everything is a bit blurred. But I am not blind. Once I put on my glasses, things become clear.

In like manner, all of us have a certain way of looking at ourselves and the world in which we live. Every one of us, in other words, has a particular set of lenses through which we interpret the reality that surrounds us and our identity and role in that context. These lenses are calibrated according to our background and experiences. For the Christian, the Bible can serve as a different and fresh set of lenses. As the Word of God, it should profoundly shape our vision of life. The Bible is the set of lenses that brings us and everything around us into focus as God would want us to perceive it. This view of the world may be at odds with the way others regard matters, but the important point is that through the Bible we as believers gain proper perspective, the angle that God desires we have on important issues.

This chapter and the two that follow probe what the Bible has to say about matters related to immigration. This information can be part of the lenses that enable Christians—both those of the majority culture and Hispanics—to process issues related to immigration in the United States today. This survey is not exhaustive, nor is it a technical exercise in biblical scholarship.[1] My goal is to demonstrate the breadth of relevant material in the Bible in order to remind all concerned that God has much to teach all of us. Some of what follows comes from Hispanic biblical studies that can shed new light on passages in ways that might surprise the reader.[2]

A Growing Concern

As the presence of Hispanics continues to grow, a variety of church bodies have begun to address immigration from an overt faith perspective. As mentioned at the close of the preceding chapter, different denominations and organizations have also made official pronouncements with respect to immigration. Additional materials are appearing in journals, books, and on the internet. The Catholic Church, in contrast to most, has a long tradition of including the migrant in its pastoral concerns. The right to migrate is connected to the church's call

44

to care for the vulnerable on the one hand, and to the human entitlement to dignity and the responsibility of providing for family on the other. There is a history of teaching that spans from, for example, Pope Pius XII's *Exsul Familia* in 1952 to Pope John Paul II's 1999 *Ecclesia in America* (paragraph 65) and his various messages on World Migration Day (a practice continued by Pope Benedict XVI); the 2004 Instruction *Erga migrantes caritas Christi*; and the declarations of the recent Fifth General Conference of Latin American and Caribbean Bishops that was celebrated with Pope Benedict XVI in Brazil in May 2007 (CELAM, *Documento de Aparecida*, paragraphs 411–16).[3] These statements and more extensive studies reference a few passages in the Old and New Testaments. Much, though, has been left unsaid.

This overview of what the Bible has to say about immigration begins at the beginning, as it were—in the book of Genesis—with the creation of man and woman in the image of God. What it means to be a human must be the foundation for any discussion. The chapter then discusses the many people of God in the Old Testament who for all kinds of reasons had to leave their home country and settle somewhere else. Migration is not a new phenomenon; it is as old as time. Chapter 3 discusses the virtue of hospitality in the Old Testament and the various laws in the Pentateuch regarding foreigners. Chapter 4 turns its attention to the New Testament.

The Image of God

Genesis 1

Above all else, immigration is the movement of *people* across borders. The bottom line is that it concerns humans: their worth, destiny, rights, and responsibilities. The Bible gives great prominence to the creation of humans. Their creation is the climax of the account in Genesis 1. It is the last step in the divine movement to organize the chaos and fill the emptiness of the earth (1:2). In the narrative, the first three days of creation involve dividing darkness from light; separating the land, water, and sky; and preparing the earth for habitation (1:3–13). On the fourth, fifth, and sixth days God places celestial bodies in the heavens, fish in the sea, and birds in the sky (1:14–25). The final piece of his handiwork is the creation of man and woman (1:26–31).

Six times the text says that God saw what he had made and that it was "good" (1:4, 10, 12, 18, 21, 25). Everything was in its proper place and functioning as it should under the sovereignty

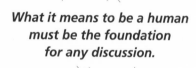

What it means to be a human must be the foundation for any discussion.

of the Creator; the whole scene teems with sanctified life. After the creation of humans, the text declares "and it was *very* good" (1:31, emphasis added). Fittingly, this is the seventh occurrence of the term *good*. Seven is a special number in the Bible and regularly represents perfection. The qualifier "very good" and the number seven together emphasize that the creation of people is the pinnacle of what God has made. Humans are special indeed.

What is it, though, that makes humans unique among the other living creatures in the created order? Verses 26 and 27 teach that every person, male and female, is made in the image of God. What does this concept of the image of God actually mean? How might this truth about humanity inform the immigration debate?

There are at least three views as to what it means to be created in the image of God.[4] The first argues that the image deals with what humans *inherently are* or *possess*. The idea is that every person has a will, intellect, emotions, and a spiritual component that distinguish them from all other creatures. Others take the position that the image should be considered *relationally*. Those who take this position believe that the only person who ever truly incarnated the image of God was Jesus (2 Cor. 4:4; Col. 1:15). Individuals who are reconciled with God through faith in him are able to participate in the image and thus regain the relationship with God that was ruptured at the fall in Genesis 3. Finally, some contend that the image of God ought to be understood in a *functional* sense. In the ancient world, kings would set up statues of themselves in far-off territories as a witness to their authority over that region. In like manner, humans, who are God's living image on earth, are designed to represent him here. This representation is not to be passive; men and women are to preside over all things as God's vice-regents and take care of his creation (Gen. 1:26, 28; 2:15, 19–20). This dominion requires wisdom, creativity, and care, and God has splendidly equipped every human for this great task.

Each of these three perspectives has a biblical basis (although the last seems to be the one most clearly stressed in Gen. 1). Each one in its own way underscores the particular value of all persons: what they intrinsically are, their potential relationship with the Creator, and their capacity and privilege as rulers. Everyone is made in God's image and therefore has a singular standing before God and in the world.

Implications for Today

Value as persons. The creation of all persons in the image of God must be the most basic conviction for Christians as they approach the challenges of immigration today. Immigration should not be argued in the abstract, because it is fundamentally about *immigrants*. Immigrants are humans, and as such they are made in God's image. Each and every one of those who have come to the United States is God's creation and is worthy of respect. Because immigrants are made in the divine image, they have an essential value and possess immense potential to contribute to society and to the common good through their presence, work, and ideas.

Human rights and the image of God. If one takes what the Bible says in Genesis 1 seriously, as revelation from God, then what it communicates about humans becomes a divine claim on Christian attitudes and actions toward those who have arrived in this country—irrespective of whether they are here with or without the documents the government might mandate. To turn away or to treat badly one made in the image of God ultimately is a violation against God. As a consequence, the topic of immigration at some level needs to be considered from a human rights perspective and not be defined solely in terms of national security, cultural identity, or economic impact. From the standpoint of national security, for example, the primary concern is to control the border. Those trying to enter the country in any manner not permitted by law are categorized logically, then, as intruders and must be kept out. In contrast, a human rights perspective has as its special focus the needs and fate of the immigrants themselves. Immigration has been treated as a human rights issue within legal theory and international law for some time.[5]

Human rights language, however, raises red flags for some people. On occasion it has been used arbitrarily by a few special-interest groups, and this makes many suspicious of any reference to human rights. Whatever may be the ideological basis of those organizations, however, the point here is a biblical one. Immigrants are made in the image of God. Believers must examine their hearts for possible contrary allegiances that might lead them to want to deny entry to those from elsewhere—whether this be on cultural, racial, socioeconomic, educational, or political grounds. Misconceptions also arise from the tendency to generalize. Some assume that all Hispanics are the same, when in fact they come from different countries, each with its own history, customs, food, and religious traditions; nor do all Hispanics come from the same racial, social, economic, educational, or even linguistic backgrounds. The image of God should lead to an appreciation of the worth and potential of Hispanics, both as a group and as individuals.

At the same time, of course, each person of the majority, or host, culture is made in the image of God, too. This fact can add an interesting element to attitudes toward those from other countries. In the Old Testament, God is portrayed as limitlessly compassionate not only toward his own people (Exod. 34:6–7; Joel 2:13) but also to those beyond the community of faith. In the book of Jonah, the prophet admits that the God of Israel would be merciful even to the Assyrians, the cruelest empire of that time (Jon. 4:2; cf. Ps. 145:8–9). His grace knows no bounds. One way those of the majority culture can reflect the divine image is to demonstrate that same compassion to others—in this case, to immigrants who have come to seek a better life in this country.

It must be made clear at this juncture that this conviction in no way implies that there should be no control over immigration or no order at the country's southern border. What the image-of-God premise does, though, is establish a basic mind-set from which one can formulate policy and evaluate pragmatic decisions that must be made in the many spheres of national life. It also should inform the tone of Christian participation in the national debate. Ultimately, immigration is about people. This is where the discussion should begin, not with disputes over legal status. This is a topic that certainly must be dealt with, yet it is not the place *to begin* the treatment of the topic of immigration. In fact, this new starting point of the image of God greatly affects the nature of any legislation that will be formulated. An appreciation of immigrants as people can lead to laws that are compassionate and empowering for the immigrant and for the common good, instead of laws that at bottom are exclusionary and largely punitive.

Expectations of the image. This word about the image of God has important things to convey to immigrant believers, too. First of all, it can be an encouragement. For many reasons, immigrants can feel inferior and of less worth. They may have less schooling, come from a more deprived economic background, have a hard time learning English or speak what they do know with an accent, and be of a different skin color or of one that is different than those in their host neighborhoods. They may not know the laws or handle cultural cues well; many live in perpetual fear of the authorities. The fact that they are made in God's image should generate a more edifying perspective about themselves—about who they are and what they can become, about what they can add to their new context and to the well-being of their communities. Whatever their previous or present condition, they are valuable before God and, therefore, to the United States.

Not surprisingly, this theme of the image of God and Hispanic identity and worth is a major topic in Hispanic theological writing. What these authors try to convey is that Hispanics have significance not only as humans in a general sense but also, just as important, *as Hispanic persons.* It is at this point that the theme of *mestizaje,* which was mentioned in the previous chapter, comes into play theologically and pastorally.[6] Ethnicity is no longer something to be ashamed of. *Mestizaje* can be embraced as a gift from God and is inseparable from being a valued human being—a unique person, one from a special people with a matchless history and culture. Immigrants have an intrinsic dignity as humans and as Hispanics.

The image of God makes a claim on Hispanics as well. The fact that immigrants are made in God's image should cause them to reflect on what his expectations of them might be. Their divine endowment has profound implications for the way they develop their capabilities in education and at the workplace; it should impact how immigrants carry out their responsibilities as potential citizens, raise their families, work at their jobs, handle their money, and generally engage the world in which they now live.[7] In addition, immigrants should value the people of this country as those made in God's image. To be easily critical of things Anglo or African American as a defensive reaction to prejudice or in order to extol the mores of Latin American cultures at the expense of others is to contradict what Hispanics themselves seek: appreciation for their backgrounds and abilities. For the Hispanic, as for the majority culture, being God's representative is both a *privilege* and a *responsibility*.

Through its instruction on the image of God, the Bible can mold the attitudes and actions of the majority culture and Hispanic Christians. For the former, it can yield fresh appreciation of the immigrants' value and promise; for the latter, its message is one of encouragement to forge ahead and an exhortation to live well as God's representatives.

The Experiences of the People of God

A second way in which the Old Testament can inform immigration discussions is through its accounts of the many people of God who moved across borders. This movement involved individuals, families, and large groups. Sometimes it was voluntary. In other instances it was forced. It is undeniable that the Old Testament is full of stories of people on the move. This is not surprising. In many ways, human history is the history of migration. So, too, is the history of God's people.

Some might contend that the Bible does not present details of the lives of immigrants but rather of refugees or deportees. Therefore, it would not be appropriate to appeal to the Scriptures for a study on immigration per se. This observation is true in a strictly technical sense with respect to some biblical passages. Nevertheless, it ignores the fact that not all the migrations recorded in the Old Testament were of refugees and deportees. More important, this argument overlooks that immigration is not only about the reasons and mechanics of the move *to* another place; it is about life *in* that new setting. In this regard, there are lessons to be gleaned from the Old Testament irrespective of *how* these persons found themselves out of their land.

Others might object to the following survey by pointing out that the accounts of the Hebrew Bible describe the expe-

Immigration is not only about the reasons and mechanics of the move *to* another place; it is about life *in* that new setting.

riences of Israel (and Judah), not of any and all immigrants. The question that has been posed to me is whether I am seeking to equate all Hispanic immigrants with God's people. The answer is no—even though there is a large multitude of believers among those who come.

The purpose of presenting this material is twofold. First, these biblical passages demonstrate how central migrations are to much of the Hebrew Bible. This awareness should alert us to how universal this phenomenon is, and it can impact our understanding of what these texts portray and teach us. Second, these accounts depict how migrant people responded to circumstances in their day. These responses are similar to what Hispanic (and all) immigrants go through. The text, in other words, can make readers more sensitive to the immigrant population and the challenges they face.

In the end, these contentions against appealing to the Bible in the immigration discussion, although trying to be faithful to the biblical text, miss the important truth of God's concern for the vulnerable. His is a deep love for the needy and disenfranchised, whoever they are and whatever the cause of their situation. His is not a selective mercy. He cares for each human, because each one, as we have seen, is made in his image. The most fundamental tenet of the Christian faith is that God loved the entire world so much that he sent his son Jesus to die for all humanity (John 3:16). The Bible also teaches that he is sovereignly involved in the movements of all peoples (Amos 9:7; cf. Acts 17:26–28). Today, this would mean that God is present in some way in the migrations we are witnessing worldwide.

What follows is organized under three general headings: hunger, forced exile, and life as foreigners. Classifying the biblical accounts in this way can lead to a better appreciation of the various reasons people in the Old Testament migrated and how they responded in each situation.

Hunger

The patriarchs. The book of Genesis recounts the stories of several migrations. Abram (he will not be called Abraham until Gen. 17:5) and his extended family leave Ur of the Chaldeans at God's command and move to Canaan (Gen. 11:31–12:9). This relocation, however, did not signify that they settled permanently in one place. The patriarch and his descendants lived a nomadic life, even in the promised land. The only piece of ground Abraham is said to have owned was the cave of Machpelah, which he bought from Ephron the Hittite in order to have a plot in which to bury his wife Sarah (Gen. 23; cf. 49:29–33). In numerous places in Genesis the patriarchs are called "sojourners" or are said to "sojourn" in an area for a time: Abraham (17:8; 20:1; 21:34; 23:4), Isaac (35:27; 37:1), Jacob (28:4; 32:4 [32:5 MT]), and Jacob's sons (47:4, 9).[8] In fact, this itinerant experience so marked Israel's identity that years later it became a part of the confession spoken by the head of the household when presenting the firstfruits of the harvest to the Lord (Deut. 26:5; cf. 1 Chron. 29:15; Ps. 39:12 [39:13 MT]).

Not too long after arriving in Canaan, Abram journeys to Egypt (Gen. 12:10–20). There is a famine in the land promised by God, and he and his family seek food. The climatic conditions in that part of the world are precarious, and nomads are particularly at risk. The patriarch abandons Canaan and looks for sustenance in Egypt. Because of the massive Nile River and the rich soil in the delta and along its banks, Egypt was considered the breadbasket of the region. Egyptians were accustomed to receiving immigrants, whether for short-term or long-term stays, although reaction to them varied. A series of defense systems were established to keep some out, but small bands continually made their way to Egypt.[9]

Abram often is criticized for presenting Sarai as his sister to the Egyptians. He is fearful for his life, as he worries that Pharaoh will want to take her. Indeed, they are related (20:12), but Abram's plan seems to compromise his moral obligation to his wife and puts his faith into question. However, reading this passage with a migration lens yields another appreciation for what Abram and Sarai do.[10] A famine had triggered their migration, and Abram, as head of his household and clan, was responsible for feeding the individuals and animals under his care. A desperate situation led to a desperate ploy. After traveling such a long way in search of food, the only alternatives were to perpetuate the deception or to turn around without hope and maybe lose the struggle to survive the hunger. Sarai is willing to put herself in danger so that all can eat. These kinds of terrible quandaries continue to characterize border-crossing stories. Women are especially vulnerable in these situations, but they take what can be horrific risks for the good of their families.

What we witness in Genesis 12 is Abram/Abraham, the father of those who now believe and trust in God (Rom. 4; Gal. 3), scheming to cross a border to eat. This does not exonerate him, but maybe the subterfuge is more understandable. He would repeat this maneuver when he comes to the territory of Abimelech, the king of the Philistines (Gen. 20).

Isaac also moves to Philistine territory because of a famine (26:1). Jacob sends his sons twice to Egypt to buy food as the shortages worsened (41:57–42:6; 43:1–7). Eventually he and his sons and their families move to Egypt. There, under Joseph's provision, they are able to escape the hunger (47:10–13). In each of these cases, the one receiving the migrant patriarch and his family is charitable and willing to meet their needs.

Ruth. Another instance of a family moving to another country in time of famine is set during the period of the judges and is found in the book of Ruth. In order to survive, Elimelech, his wife Naomi, and their two sons leave Bethlehem in Judah. They cross the Jordan to dwell in the plains of Moab, and there the sons marry Moabite women (Ruth 1:1–2). Within a span of just a few verses, the narrative provides a second example of migration, literally in the opposite direction. Elimelech dies after the arrival in Moab, and within ten years his sons die, too (1:3–5). The three widows are left to provide for themselves. Naomi had heard that the Lord was providing food for his people in Bethlehem, so she and one of her daughters-in-law, Ruth, go back to Naomi's hometown (1:6–19). The other, Orpah, remains in Moab.

These two solitary women—one an Israelite, the other a foreign dependent related by marriage—return, but they struggle to make ends meet. Their situations are now reversed: Naomi the immigrant has come home; Ruth, who had married an outsider, becomes an immigrant in a strange land. The younger woman goes to the fields every day to gather food to support her Israelite mother-in-law and herself. Eventually her hard work and stellar character incur the favor of Naomi's kinsman, Boaz. He redeems Naomi's property and marries Ruth. Through Boaz's marriage to this Moabite and the son born of that relationship, the ancestral land is able to remain within the family. Boaz fulfills his familial obligation to Naomi, but he does not do this grudgingly. Boaz is generous to Ruth, an immigrant woman in need, even though she is a Moabite to whom the law was less than favorable (Num. 22–25; Deut. 23:3), and he extends protection and provision to her through marriage.

The book of Ruth can be read in many rich ways. Studies on the legal background concerning the gleaning, property, and inheritance shed light on the account's details. It can be appreciated, too, as an exemplary lesson in mercy and faithfulness, both between individuals and as a sovereign blessing from God.[11]

The book can also be read as an immigrant story.[12] Assimilation theory can be helpful here.[13] This approach looks at how immigrants acquire the requisite sociocultural competencies to move into their new context. It proposes that there are three kinds of mechanisms needed to succeed: purposive action, networks and forms of human capital, and institutional avenues.

As to the first, Ruth makes her famous declaration that she will return to Bethlehem with Naomi (1:14–18). There is an interesting dynamic at this point in the narrative. Naomi exhorts her two daughters-in-law to go back to their families (1:8–13). Why does Ruth decide not to return to her people like Orpah? Would her status as a childless widow of a foreigner have carried a stigma? One wonders, too, why Naomi says nothing when Ruth states that she will leave all and cling to her mother-in-law. There is no acknowledgment, no expression of gratitude for this selfless decision. Is part of Naomi's bitterness (1:15, 20–21) directed at Moab, the place where her husband and sons died? How does she evaluate what Ruth has done? The reader can only speculate. Other purposive actions taken by Ruth include her initiative to glean, her interaction with Boaz in chapter 2, and her actions at the threshing floor in chapter 3, which could have backfired horribly and left her with a bad reputation.

Engaging the networks in Bethlehem, the second component in the assimilation process, brings another set of challenges for Ruth. She has to interact with and gain the acceptance of the town's women, the reapers, and the elders, as well as navigate the foreign environment of her new dwelling with her mother-in-law. Things do not seem to begin well. When she and Naomi arrive, she is not introduced to the townsfolk. Has Naomi ignored her? Is she embarrassed by the presence of a Moabite daughter-in-law? After all, the Moabites were portrayed negatively in Israelite tradition (Gen. 19:30–37; Num. 22–25; Deut. 23:3–6 [MT 23:4–7]). Perhaps because of this fact, the women of Bethlehem do not engage Ruth. Was there awkwardness in that scene, both for Naomi and Ruth? In chapter 2 the workers single her out as an outsider (was it her clothing? an accent?), although they appreciate her perseverance (2:7). Ruth calls herself a "foreigner" (2:10) and a "servant" (2:13). Does she feel out of place and uncomfortable? No one knows her name; perhaps no one had even asked. She is simply an outsider, the woman who returned with Naomi (2:6).

Boaz immediately is supportive. He values Ruth (2:11–12), shares food with her, and allows her to gather freely (2:14–18). In chapter 3 he accepts his role as kinsman-redeemer and sends her on her way with more food. By the end of chapter 4 Ruth is married and has won the respect of the elders. They compare her to Rachel and Leah, two women from outside the land who played significant roles in Israel's history (4:11–12). The women, who had not noticed (or maybe ignored) Ruth at her arrival, praise God for the child and encourage Naomi with her loyalty (4:14–15).

What of Naomi? Naomi is still silent and does not respond to the women's words. But she does embrace Ruth's son, Obed.

The one who bemoaned that she had come back empty (1:20–21) now has someone to care for her in her old age, and she will care for him (4:15–17). Surely this boy from a bicultural marriage would not experience what his immigrant mother had, nor would he have to try like she had done to gain entry into the life of that place. It would be home for him from the start. Bethlehem, too, would be a different place after its inclusion of this Moabite woman and her son, probably with a new appreciation of the people who lived on the other side of the Dead Sea.

The third component of assimilation theory is the institutional avenues. In the case of Ruth, these are the pertinent laws mentioned above, related to gleaning, inheritance, the redemption of property, and perhaps levirate marriage. Her actions in the story suggest that she is aware of these and applies them to her situation.

Is Ruth able to accommodate herself to Bethlehem? Does she find full acceptance? The reader can sense that the ethnic boundaries do not totally disappear. The townspeople never call Ruth by name. To the reapers she is simply the "Moabite" (2:6); to those at the gate she is "the woman" (4:11) and "this young woman" (4:12); to the women of the town, "your daughter-in-law" (4:15). Even Boaz in public refers to her as "Ruth the Moabite" (4:5, 10).

Whatever her personal level of integration into that Judean town, the genealogy of the final verses of the book reveals that her story is connected to the lineage of David (4:17b–22). In her wildest imaginings could she ever have dreamed that her experiences were part of something so significant? In the New Testament she appears in the genealogy of Jesus (Matt. 1:5)! What is more, every year Jews read the book of Ruth for the Feast of Weeks (Shavuot) and commemorate this peasant woman's life. This life—the striving and hardships of an immigrant—was a key element in the plan of God.

Forced Exile

Joseph. In addition to cases of migration to other places in search of food and water, there are instances where individuals or groups are forced to leave the land against their will. In the book of Genesis, Joseph is sold by his brothers to passing Midianite traders. These in turn take him to Egypt and sell him to Potiphar, an officer of Pharaoh (Gen. 37:28, 36). This unfortunate immigrant, in a place not of his own choosing and far from his family, proved to be a faithful worker with high moral standards. But Joseph's uprightness is of no avail, as he is wrongly accused of molesting his master's wife and put in prison (Gen. 39). Whose word would the authorities believe? That of an important Egyptian, or that of a foreigner? In jail Joseph confirms his integrity and wisdom, and after his release he is promoted to be governor over Egypt, one of the most powerful nations in the world (Gen. 40–41). This immigrant ends up saving the nation from famine (Gen. 47).

Joseph accommodates himself to Egyptian life in a variety of ways. When he is to be brought before Pharaoh, he is shaved according to Egyptian custom (41:14). The ceremonial promotion of Joseph also fits that context (41:41–43). He is given an Egyptian name and marries an Egyptian woman, with whom he has two sons; the Israelite names of his sons indicate, though, that he has forgotten neither his God nor his home (41:45, 50–52). Joseph adopts the dress and makeup commensurate with his social station to such an extent that his brothers do not recognize him (43:8; 45:1–15). Joseph observes another cultural convention when he serves them food: it was not permitted for Egyptians to eat with the Hebrews, and so his brothers are served separately (43:32). Clearly Joseph speaks Egyptian. He uses the ruse of having a translator present when speaking to his brothers, but he understands them (42:23–24). This immigrant, in other words, had not forgotten his mother tongue. The inner tensions of this transplanted Israelite surface again when Joseph dies. He is embalmed and placed in a coffin, according to Egyptian practice (50:26; cf. 50:3), but before his death Joseph declares his longing to return to his land (50:24–25; cf. Exod. 13:19; Josh. 24:32).

The respect and affection Joseph earned from the Egyptians is made manifest when they share his grief at Jacob's death (Gen. 50:4–14). From archaeological reliefs and inscriptions we learn that Egypt assimilated many foreigners into their economic, social, military, and political spheres.[14] Joseph is an illustration of this openness; at the same time, he is an example of the conflicted nature of many immigrants throughout the ages, who struggle with a heart for two cultures—the home culture and that of the host country.

Daniel. Joseph is not the only person deported from his homeland who served in a high position in the government of another country. Another is Daniel. He was taken from Jerusalem along with other promising young men by the Babylonian king Nebuchadnezzar (Dan. 1:1–4a). Babylonian foreign policy entailed taking the best of the leadership from conquered territories and retraining them for posts within the imperial bureaucracy. During his time in Babylon, Daniel served four kings of two empires: the Babylonians Nebuchadnezzar and Belshazzar, and the Persians Darius and Cyrus (Dan. 1–6). Throughout his long tenure this immigrant statesman steadfastly maintained his faith in the Lord and on several occasions was willing to sacrifice his life rather than compromise his beliefs. His uprightness was applauded by several of these kings.

From the very beginning Daniel has to determine the appropriate level of accommodation to Babylonian culture, not only in a general sense but also within the charged political atmosphere of the national palace as one from a defeated people. The program to which he and his friends are assigned was designed to prepare them to better serve the empire. It involved teaching them a new language, reeducating them in the literature and ways of Babylon, providing them a different diet, and giving them Babylonian names—all important components of cultural identity (1:4b–7). Commentaries often remark that Daniel and his three friends refused to compromise on the food because of the strictures of Jewish dietary law and that this refusal demonstrates the strength of their faith. This is true theologically,

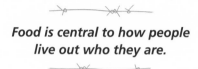

**Food is central to how people
live out who they are.**

but what is missed is the very thing cultural studies would underscore: food is central to how people live out who they are. One has only to look at the ethnic restaurants and grocery stores in immigrant communities or how American tourists look for McDonald's to recognize how integral food is to self-definition. To maintain a separate diet in Daniel's case would be pleasing to the Lord because of its religious meaning, yes, but it would also be a tangible way for their keepers to recognize their particular cultural boundaries (1:8–16). Another cultural marker was his prayer life and faithfulness to his God. During his tenure his faith was mocked (Dan. 5), and his stance got him thrown into the lions' den (6:5–16).

Deportees and refugees. The biblical text also mentions the removal or the flight of many others, but oftentimes these people are not named in the biblical accounts. They are the masses who are the helpless victims of the cruelties of war and the material want that comes in its aftermath. When Samaria, the capital of the northern kingdom, was sacked by the Assyrians in 722 BC and attacked a second time in 720 BC, thousands were forcibly carried off to different parts of the empire (2 Kings 17:1–6, 23; 18:9–11). Archaeological finds reveal a sudden surge in the population of the southern kingdom of Judah in the last quarter of the eighth century BC, probably the result of a major flow southward of refugees fleeing the Assyrian onslaught.[15] A few years later (701 BC), another Assyrian king, Sennacherib, laid siege to Jerusalem. Even though unable to subjugate the city, in his annals Sennacherib claims to have taken away a large number of prisoners and booty from his war against Judah.[16] When the city was put under siege by King Nebuchadnezzar of Babylon for the first time in 597 BC, ten thousand were deported (2 Kings 24:14–16). Jerusalem finally fell a decade later (587/586 BC). What remained of the elite and a few thousand others were sent away (2 Kings 25:6–7, 11, 21; 2 Chron. 36:18, 20; Jer. 52:27–31). We will return to the description of the life of these deportees below.

Escapees. There are examples, too, of individuals who flee to another country in order to save their lives.[17] Several are prominent figures in biblical history. Moses escaped from Egypt after killing a taskmaster (Exod. 2:11–14). He settled in Midian for forty years. He must have integrated into that community over those decades, learning their language and customs (note the respect he shows Jethro, Exod. 18). There he married Zipporah (2:15–22), but when they had a son, Moses named him Gershom, saying "I have become a foreigner in a foreign land" (2:22). The boy's name is a word play on the Hebrew *gēr* ("foreigner"), a key term that will be examined in the next chapter. Apparently, Moses's foreign roots still ran deep. He had grown up in Pharaoh's court, and his name is probably of Egyptian origin (although this is a point of contention among scholars). Moses was given an education worthy of his social standing (2:5–10; cf. Heb. 11:23–27). The skills in leadership and the military arts learned in the royal palace would prepare him for the role he would later have in leading the Israelites out of Egypt.[18] The training and migrant experiences of this foreigner, in other words, were an important part of God's plan to free his people. Ironically, his assimilation process in due course moves in still another direction—from the adopted Egyptian and Midianite contexts to his Israelite roots. Moses needed both the Egyptian and Israelite cultures (including their languages) to engage Pharaoh and his court and to fulfill his divine calling to guide his people to the promised land. His time in the remote areas of Midian prepared him for the wilderness wandering.

Similarly, David had to run from Saul. For a time he lived among the Philistines (1 Sam. 27), and he took his parents to Moab for their safety (22:3–4). Jeroboam went down to Egypt to get away from Solomon, who sought to kill him after Jeroboam received the prophetic word from Ahijah that he would be king over ten of Israel's tribes (1 Kings 11:29–40; 12:2–3). Jeremiah and his scribe Baruch were taken to Egypt by those who were involved in the assassination of the Babylonian governor Gedaliah. Gedaliah had been appointed by the king of Babylon to rule over the region after the fall of Jerusalem. The conspirators and their followers feared the vengeance of the empire, and, even though the prophet told them that they should trust the Lord and stay, they fled to Egypt and took him with them (Jer. 40–44).

Life as Foreigners

The Old Testament not only provides accounts of the plight of those taken to other countries and of those who had been forced to flee; it also describes the life of their descendants in those faraway lands. There are two central historical experiences of the people of God staying in other places for long periods: the sojourn in Egypt and the exile in Assyria and Babylon.

Egypt. The beginning of the account in the book of Exodus is far removed from the days of Joseph. In those days, Pharaoh had allowed entry to Jacob and his family and graciously received them out of respect for Joseph (Gen. 47:1–12). There are glimpses of prejudice, however, in the narrative. Initially Joseph does not eat with his brothers because of this (43:32), and then the Israelites are sent to Goshen, as the Egyptians found shepherds detestable (46:34). Certain passages inform us that the Israelites' stay in Egypt lasted about four hundred years (15:13; cf. Acts 7:6). For an undisclosed time the Israelites experienced protection under Joseph and those who had known him, but then they were reduced to slavery (Exod. 1:8). As slaves, they worked on royal building projects and in agriculture (1:11–14).

Even as they benefited from the Israelites' toil, Pharaoh and the Egyptians feared the surprising increase in the number of the Israelites (1:9–13, 20; 5:5). They were willing to take advantage of the cheap labor of this foreign people as long as they were "invisible." Once the population of Israelites increased, however, the Egyptians began to worry. They took measures to control this growth, to the point of decreeing state-sponsored infanticide (1:15–2:4), but there never was any question of curtailing their labor or alleviating their work. The response to complaints and insubordination was to prescribe higher and more difficult quotas (5:6–21). The empire needed these foreigners to complete their construction projects and to work the fields to feed its populace. Life for the Israelites was hard and their overlords cruel. This description agrees with extrabiblical evidence of Semites serving as slaves in ancient Egypt.[19]

In the midst of their suffering the Israelites cry out to God, and God answers (2:23–25). The structure of the narrative in Exodus is instructive. Before the lament of the people is recorded, Moses is placed in Midian (2:15–22), where he would receive the revelation at the burning bush (3:1–10). The plan of God, in other words, had already been set in motion. Under Moses they would go to Canaan, where they could live as a free people in a new place that offered them a better quality of existence, a "land flowing with milk and honey" (3:8, 17). There they would have their own homes and vineyards, a blessing denied them as slaves (Deut. 6:11; Josh. 24:13). The rest of the Pentateuch is the story of how they reached the border of that promised land. How profound the impact of Egyptian culture was on the Israelites is evident, though, by their pining for the food of that land of servitude (Exod. 16:3).

Assyria and Babylon. The second setting for life in another region described in some detail in the Old Testament is the exile in Babylon after the defeat of Judah. While some had been carried away before that time (such as Daniel and Ezekiel, among others), a final deportation took place after the destruction of Jerusalem. The Old Testament contains a lot of material that portrays the fate and feelings of the Judeans in Babylon. It is silent, however, about the Israelites who had been taken earlier by the Assyrians from the northern kingdom in 722 and 720 BC and from Judah in 701 BC. In a fortuitous turn of events, archaeologists have discovered inscriptional data and reliefs that provide information about the life of deportees in the Neo-Assyrian Empire.[20]

Administrative documents reveal that the fortunes of individuals and of families were quite varied. Much depended on the skills these persons might have and what the particular needs of the empire were at the moment. Those who were carpenters or smiths fared fairly well, as did those who were put into government positions. Some troops and charioteers were absorbed into the imperial armies; other deportees apparently were merchants. The less fortunate were conscripted into service as domestics or were assigned to harsh labor on farms or on building projects. Some assimilation appears to have taken place, and one would expect that this process would have differed according to circumstances and social standing. That this occurred is evident by data suggesting that later generations took non-Israelite names. It also would have been necessary to acquire the language of their captors; intermarriage was inevitable.

The Old Testament portrayal of life in Babylon is extensive, covering the fate of the royal family to that of the more common people.[21] It was customary to have captured kings live in the palace. They were viewed as living trophies, and their treatment depended on the good graces of the victorious monarch. Jehoiachin, who was a victim of Nebuchadnezzar's siege of 597 BC, was taken along with his family and officials (2 Kings 24:10–16). The book of 2 Kings closes with a notice of his eventual promotion among the other defeated kings. The Babylonians considered him to be the last legitimate ruler of Judah (25:27–30). He was given a seat of honor at the table of Awel-Marduk, Nebuchadnezzar's son, and provided new clothes and a stipend. Fate was not as kind to Zedekiah. After Jerusalem had been taken, his sons were killed and his eyes gouged out; he was then carried away in chains (25:6–7). He is not heard of again.

The text offers glimpses of the feelings of some of the recent arrivals in Babylon. Psalm 137 is a lament that expresses the pain over loss, above all over the ruin of Jerusalem—with its palace, the symbol of the Davidic dynasty and hope of glory, and the temple, the special place of God's dwelling and the center of their faith. There is sorrow, shame, and anger; it is a veritable roller coaster of emotions about being so far from everything that gave meaning and order to life. Some exiles expected a quick return. Indeed, a few prophets had announced as much (Jer. 28). But Jeremiah sends a letter to the exiles and tells them that their stay in Babylon will be a long one, at least seventy years (Jer. 29). The letter is interesting, because it counsels them to invest in their new land. They are to build houses, plant gardens, marry and raise families, and pray for God's blessing on that place (29:5–7). We do not know how many of those in Babylon received this communication.

Ezekiel lived and ministered among the exiles (Ezek. 1:1–2; 2:15), but he does not mention Jeremiah. The fact that there are elders still functioning within the community of exiles is an indication that the people enjoyed some level of autonomy in their daily lives.

Return to the land. It is clear that the hope of a return to the promised land burned in the hearts of many of the Jews in exile. Testimony to this fact is the series of returns from Babylon, first under Zerubbabel (Ezra 1–3; cf. Neh. 7), then under Ezra (Ezra 7–8), and last under Nehemiah (Neh. 2). This does not mean, however, that there had been no adjustments made to the majority culture in Babylon. Before he returns to Jerusalem, Nehemiah had risen to a place of prominence and unique trust as the king's cupbearer (Neh. 1:11). He must have absorbed the language, customs, and political protocols to have achieved that position (as in the case of Daniel earlier). Still, he maintains a strong bond to the land of his fathers (1:1–4) and his faith in God (1:5–11; 2:4–5). By contrast, Ezra, as a priest, naturally holds his cultural-religious boundaries tightly and is recognized as a religious leader of another people by the Persian authorities (Ezra 7:1–12, 21, 25).

The dynamic of the move back is complex.[22] The books of Ezra and Nehemiah demonstrate that it involved more than a geographical change. The return was part of a larger set of commitments, tightly bound to the ancient traditions. Surely there were idealized (and probably unrealistic) expectations of what going "home" would be like. Upon arrival, there were issues revolving around legitimacy (hence, the genealogies); the reclaiming of the holy place and the reinstitution of proper ritual (the rebuilding of the altar and the temple, the celebration of Passover); a concern for protection (the need to rebuild the wall); and the fear of cultural loss and lapsing into disobedience, uncleanness, and a social ethos divergent from the demands of the law. Lineage, religious life, ethical commitments, language, and marital boundaries were all part of the returnees' cultural self-definition—and preservation. Although the handling of the challenge of the mixed marriages in Ezra 9–10 and Nehemiah 13:23–31 appears harsh at this remove from that context, perhaps this backdrop of the cultural needs and sensibilities of migrants returning to their land after so many years, with all of what that would have represented, can help explain the measures that were taken.[23]

What sustained them, too, was hope. Prophetic words had assured them that, even though they were a defeated people and an insignificant minority within an empire, the Lord their God was mightier than the deities of Babylon and any other political power (e.g., Isa. 40–55; Dan. 2–7). He was able to bring them back, irrespective of the obstacles in the journey, which was a migration back to their homeland.[24] Haggai and Zechariah stood beside them as they built a new temple. These prophets and others in the past had foretold the coming of a king who would rule over a restored Israel and over all the nations in justice and peace (Isa. 9, 11, 32; Jer. 33; Ezek. 36–48; Hag. 2; Zech. 9). The expectation was that things would be different from what they had been for so long.

Their identity as Jews would be experienced in a different way. Those who returned were not the same people. They had seen the world and the great cities of its most powerful empires. They had lived among other cultures and participated in different ways of life within a context so unlike their own. Going back to the land was a return to the same place, but the returnees and even that place called "home" had changed. The opposition they endured, such as what Ezra and Nehemiah faced from within and without the community, may have been due to the competing agendas and aspirations of those who did not want to see the status quo changed. There would have been some suspicion and resentment toward the newly arrived on the part of those who had remained in the land. It would not be surprising if economic status were at play, and there would have been differences of opinion as to how best to engage the ruling Persian authorities and comply with imperial demands (Neh. 4–6, 13).[25] How had the dreams and aspirations of those in exile been fulfilled and/or challenged, even shattered?

Persia. Not everyone went back to the land. Many stayed behind.[26] The story of Esther is a special case in point. There is no inkling that either she or her kinsman Mordecai had given any thought of living anywhere else. There is the tension in the narrative of their being part of the larger society as members of a marginalized community.

Cultural accommodation percolates under the surface. Even though Mordecai is a Jew of the tribe of Benjamin, his name is probably connected to Marduk, the chief god of Babylon. Recent discoveries demonstrate that it was a common name, so no religious significance is necessarily attached to it. The point is that it is not an Israelite name. Perhaps he had two names, the other a Hebrew one, as did his relative Esther (see below). Mordecai denounces a plot to kill the king (Esther 2:19–23). Was this out of loyalty and appreciation to the crown? Apparently, Mordecai was doing well financially, too. Several times the text says that he sits at the king's gate (2:19, 21; 3:2; 5:9, 13; 6:10, 12). This might be an indication of his stature, as normally men of importance would be found there. This also could explain Haman's anger. If Mordecai were poor and unimportant, his lack of deference would not have been so insulting. Haman's hateful and exaggerated reaction of stigmatizing all of Mordecai's ethnicity, the Jews in this case (3:6–14), is not an uncommon nativistic reaction against foreign groups.

Esther has two names: the Hebrew name Hadassah and the Babylonian or Persian name Esther (2:7). She is chosen among all the young women of the empire to replace Queen Vashti and is assigned by King Xerxes (also called Ahasuerus) to the royal harem (2:1–18).[27] Esther quickly learns the ways of the palace and eventually how to manipulate the king by organizing fabulous feasts. Whatever faith the two of them may have had is only subtly communicated by Mordecai's famous line, "And who knows but that you have come to your royal position for such a time as this" (4:14) and Esther's call for a fast (4:15–16; cf. 4:3).[28] The first hints at a trust in the sovereignty of the Lord; the second is common religious practice. At the same time, the words of Mordecai in 4:14 may be taken as prodding her to step forward to protect her people. Her initial silence (2:10) turns into a courageous plan. The rest of the account presents the growing sense of her identity and responsibility to them as one in a position in the palace. Esther in the end does reveal her background (8:5–6).

This immigrant population was spared (and a measure of revenge against their enemies was attained, 9:5–17). This event is the basis of the Jewish festival of Purim (9:18–32), which is celebrated to this day. The Jewish community in that part of the world—now modern-day Iraq—would flourish for centuries. One of its enduring contributions to Judaism is the Babylonian Talmud. Only a handful of Jews remain there today.[29]

Implications for Today

Realism and everyday life. The Old Testament is full of accounts of people who are on the move or have settled in other places. Many reasons are given for this movement, and these migrations—whether of individuals or of large groups—span centuries. They are part of the fabric of biblical history—and ours. This realization offers a lesson to the majority culture. Migrations are a recurring phenomenon. Accordingly, Hispanic immigration to the United States is but another chapter in the very long book of the annals of humankind. That being the case, one can step back and try to appreciate why people, then and now, are compelled to go to another place.

The text gives a human face to migrants. They are tested and discriminated against; they want to have a home and provide for their families; they worship God; they work at different jobs, some not by their own choice; others are gifted in special ways, rise to positions of authority, and do marvelous things for the country in which they live; some long to return to their homeland, while others choose to stay in their new context; those who do go back encounter a much more complicated situation than they probably imagined; all wrestle with how to coordinate their backgrounds with the different culture that surrounds them—the issues of language, customs, faith, politics, economics, and laws. These are also flawed individuals. They are imperfect in all kinds of ways.

In other words, the Bible offers the reader very realistic scenes and situations and amazingly true-to-life characters. These immigrants and refugees are *people* above all else, people caught up in the trials, tribulations, and joys of life. It is *everyday life*, but the text teaches that these lives are set against a much bigger canvas. These people are part of the plan of God for the unfolding of world history and the divine mission. The Old Testament recounts the reaction of the host cultures to their presence. Some individuals are compassionate, others cruel toward these foreigners. Herein are examples of immigrants and host people, good and bad, to be followed and avoided.

A creative space. Another fascinating point to ponder is the wealth of biblical books of assorted genres that were produced by those living outside the promised land. Being away from the familiar proved to be a creative space for thinking about God, life, the direction of history, and the nature of hope. Those truths still speak to us today, whatever our context. Perhaps there is a lesson in this. There is much we can learn about the Christian faith from immigrants, from those outsiders whose pilgrimage with God has been on another path.

Analogous situations. For today's immigrants, this Old Testament material can serve other ends. It has the potential to be a divine mirror, where they see themselves and identify with its descriptions and the experiences of its characters. Immigrants can actually "live" the text's scenes, because they have gone through similar experiences and have dealt with comparable emotions, tensions, and challenges.

Many immigrants seek a "promised land" of a better existence, a "land of milk and honey." But the trek here is hard, and life once they get to the United States can be full of long hours of work with low pay and few benefits. Perhaps they have left one Egypt for another. Here the majority culture fears their numbers and their being different, although it wants their labor.

Hispanic theologians emphasize the exile as the most appropriate paradigm for understanding the Hispanic situation.[30] The United States is the place to which they literally have moved,

These immigrants and refugees are people above all else, people caught up in the trials, tribulations, and joys of life.

and they sense the separation from their home country quite concretely. This is an exile not in the sense that they are here as refugees or deportees; it is an exile because conditions in their home country compelled them to leave. And so they arrive from Mexico, Puerto Rico, Cuba, Guatemala, El Salvador, and elsewhere in the Americas. But it is not the same for another group of Hispanics. In contrast to the recent arrivals, they have been here as long as they can remember, and millions are second- or third-generation descendants of immigrants. Theirs is not a physical exile but rather an interior one.

The backgrounds and experiences of Hispanics are infinitely diverse, but for all, life here is new, different, and difficult. Like the people of the Bible, they wrestle with language, other ways of doing things, an unknown political system and set of laws, and marginalization. What is "home"? Where is it? Who are they? What might it mean to "seek the peace and prosperity of the city" (Jer. 29:7) today and in this place?[31] What are the appropriate parameters of accommodation or assimilation to this country? How deep will be their emotional, familial, social, and economic investment? That process will be different for each person and family. There is a wonderful title to a book in Spanish that captures this engagement between text and context so powerfully: *en la dispersión, el texto es patria* ("in the diaspora, the text is the home country").[32] The Bible, in other words, is where Hispanics can find themselves and God in their "exile."

But if what immigrants see in the text is themselves, then—if that seeking is honest—what they also see are sinners. It will not do to idealize their situation or culture; the Old Testament does not do this. Its realism reminds us that the movement of peoples is not tidy and that any group is a mixed lot.

In the Bible's richness, much is available for the majority culture and for the immigrant. To the former it reveals that migration is a human condition to be appreciated and demands a response of grace. For those who are sojourners there is much to ponder there about life and faith. The text is a mirror in which is found similar experiences as well as a candid view of immigrant life.

Conclusion

This chapter has covered a lot of ground. It began with the theme of the image of God and what it means to be human. This must be the place where all Christians begin any discussion about immigration. The next major section rehearsed the many instances of migration in the Old Testament and pointed out their different causes. It also discussed the variety of cultural and faith responses of both migrants and host peoples.

The complicated picture in the text is very real. Today the situation is complicated, too! This is good news. The Bible is complex enough to connect with the realities of human life. If its depictions are so true to life, as the Word of God it can also orient believers of the majority culture and the immigrant community about the proper attitudes and perspectives with which both sides should engage the national debate.

The next chapter continues the exploration of the Old Testament. It will locate the treatment of the immigrant within the general ethos of hospitality that was common in the ancient world as it appears in the Bible. The second section will detail the legislation concerning foreigners in Israel's law. Attitudes are important, but sooner or later any society must regulate itself in concrete ways. It is no different in our world today.

3

The Law and the Sojourner
Guidance from the Old Testament, Part II

> Give me your tired, your poor,
> Your huddled masses yearning to breathe free,
> The wretched refuse of your teeming shore.
> Send these, the homeless, tempest-tost, to me,
> I lift my lamp beside the golden door!

These immortal words come from a poem written by Emma Lazarus titled "The New Colossus." It was written in 1883 to help in the effort to raise money for the construction of the pedestal for the Statue of Liberty in New York harbor. The statue had been commissioned as a French gift to commemorate the centennial of American independence in 1876 but was not completed until 1886. It was not until 1903, though, that Lazarus's poem was engraved on a plaque and placed inside the pedestal.

Over the years, and not infrequently in the current debate, these lines have been used to claim that the Statue of Liberty stands as a powerful symbol of the fact that the United States is a nation of immigrants. Some dispute this view.[1] I will not contest the repudiation of the immigrant interpretation; it is enough for me to emphasize that at the very least this 130-year-old memorial and this poem communicate a charitable openness, an ethos of national hospitality to the vulnerable.

This notion of generous hospitality toward others pervades the Old Testament. As the previous chapter emphasized, attitudes are fundamental to how one views and treats the stranger. This chapter opens with a brief exploration of the ethics of hospitality in ancient Israel. The second section surveys Old Testament laws concerning immigrants and other foreigners. In the end, attitudes toward immigrants must be made concrete and systematized in legislation that defines their obligations and rights and that regulates the actions of the majority culture toward them. It was no different in Israel. It is the same today.

Hospitality in the Ancient World

Old Testament Practices

Travel in Old Testament times could be treacherous. There were potential dangers to be faced on the road, and there was the problem of finding sufficient food and drink and a safe haven en route. The cultures of the ancient Near East responded to these needs with shared conventions of hospitality toward the stranger. There were protocols and expectations for the host to be openhanded and for visitors not to abuse their welcome. It was assumed, too, that this act of kindness would be reciprocated if and when the host journeyed to the guest's land.

Israel was not an exception to this widespread cultural ethic.[2] Perhaps the most notable example of this practice in the Old Testament is Abraham's interaction with the three strangers who appear at his tent in Genesis 18. The patriarch comes out to greet them and immediately offers them the best refreshment he can before they continue on their way. Scenes of liberal hospitality also occur in Genesis 24, when Rebekah's brother Laban offers food to Abraham's servant and provision for his camels; in Exodus 2, where the Midianite Ruel chastises his daughters for not inviting the "Egyptian" Moses to have something to eat; and in 2 Kings 4, with the care given to Elisha by the Shunammite couple. How self-sacrificing this commitment to others could be is exemplified by the poor widow of Zarephath, who is willing to share what little she has for herself and her son with the prophet Elijah (1 Kings 17).

There are also cases where things go terribly wrong: Lot invites Abraham's guests, who have come to Sodom, into his home, but then is willing to sacrifice his daughters to protect the strangers (Gen. 19); in the second half of Judges 19 the Levite refuses to try the hospitality of Jebus (that is, Jerusalem) because it is not an Israelite city, and instead goes on to Gibeah, with horrific consequences.

Hospitality to the stranger is a virtue. Job cites his care of the traveler as testimony to his integrity (Job 31:32), and in the

**_Hospitality to the
stranger is a virtue._**

book of Isaiah hospitality to the homeless is lifted up as proof of true faith in God (Isa. 58:6–7). Some even understand Psalm 23 to contain an allusion to the custom of hospitality (v. 5). If this interpretation is correct, then graciousness toward those in need is revealed to be an attribute of the Lord himself. It is no wonder, then, that this same charitable spirit and material sharing are expected to characterize the people of God. Whatever might have been the common cultural impulse to be hospitable to the stranger in ancient times is here given a more profound motivation. To be hospitable is to imitate God.

Implications for Today

The host. In the United States it seems as if it is becoming more and more difficult to be hospitable, to take the time to be with others and welcome them into one's home. Life is so busy and full of activity, and families can be so fractured, that few are able to slow down and open their heart and hearth to anyone, let alone someone different. Nevertheless, to cling to a chosen lifestyle and schedule, define the permitted parameters of a neighborhood, and monopolize time just for oneself and one's family to the exclusion of the stranger—any stranger—might be rebellion against God and an ignoring of something dear to him. The biblical challenge to be hospitable to the stranger is set before the individual Christian and Christian communities, whether large or small.

The theme of hospitality is relevant to the immigration debate. The biblical text can gently prod believers of the majority culture to a greater mind-set of hospitality and to actions of hospitality toward the strangers who are Hispanic immigrants. To be sure, there are other strangers among the normal day-to-day contacts of the majority culture. These could be a visitor at church, a neighbor, or someone at work. But there is an immense group of other strangers who cannot be ignored. What I am not doing here (and what I cannot do) is defining what shape that hospitality should take. It can take an infinite number of forms, from small gestures of greeting or sharing a meal to broader-scale concrete action through a ministry or organization directed toward the needs of immigrants. The key is having an attitude of hospitality, a gracious spirit, toward these strangers. Might not majority-culture Christians set an example in this for the rest of the nation?

The recipient. The call to hospitality cannot be limited to the majority culture. Biblically, there is the expectation that the sojourner will not abuse the hospitality that is extended. Sadly, there are cases of immigrants who do take advantage of national and local social services and of well-meaning individuals for personal gain. There is also a criminal element within the Hispanic community (as there is in any community). These constitute a small percentage within the immigrant population, but they are the ones to whom opponents of immigration point, and they are the ones who appear on the nightly news. In this country, where a good portion of the majority culture is nervous and skeptical, this negative face of the Hispanic immigrant must be acknowledged. At the same time, and most importantly, the appreciation of the greater part of immigrants toward the United States needs to be communicated to the majority culture. I have been in prayer meetings with Hispanic pastors and Christians where, as a people of God, we have lifted up prayers of thanksgiving for the United States and for the opportunities it has afforded immigrants. This is the proper response of the beneficiary of hospitality, and it is pervasive among Hispanic believers.

If hospitality is important in the Old Testament, it is fundamental to the message of the New Testament as well. We will return to this theme and its possible lessons for today in the next chapter.

Legislation concerning the Sojourner

Hospitality functions primarily at the personal and familial level and on an informal basis. Its practice could suggest that a people have an openhandedness about them. A test of this possibility is to examine their laws and the structures of their society to ascertain whether the moral qualities of charitable welcome and kindness toward the outsider find formal expression. Do they impact how the society actually operates?

Law in the Old Testament

Misunderstandings. Many Christians have a distorted view of Old Testament law. Based on a certain reading of some verses in the Pauline Epistles, they hold to two erroneous presuppositions. First, for many, the Old Testament law equals sacrifices for sin, nothing more. This is wrong on several counts. To begin with, there are sacrifices that do not concern forgiveness of sin (such as the grain and fellowship offerings in Lev. 2–3; 6:14–23; 7:11–26). In addition, and I will discuss this a bit later, the law touches many areas of life beyond the religious rituals of ancient Israel.

The second misunderstanding is that Jews since the time of Moses (and especially in Jesus's day) believed that they had to obey the law in order to earn the right to be the people of God. The thought is that theirs was a religion only of works, while Christians are freed from the unforgiving demands of that law and can proclaim that salvation is by God's grace through faith alone.

I do not disagree with the good news of the gospel, but this perspective reveals a flawed notion of what the Old Testament law is and how it works. For a more correct appreciation, it is helpful to look at the narrative where the law is given to Israel. The flow of that account makes it unmistakably plain that the law was not intended to provide a way for the nation to gain a relationship with God.

Narrative context of the law. In Exodus 19 the people of God under the guidance of Moses have come to a mountain in the desert of Sinai. There they will receive this unique revelation from the Lord. Note when this happens. Israel had already celebrated the Passover in Egypt, in which their firstborn had been spared divine judgment by the blood of the lambs they had sprinkled on the doorposts of their homes (Exod. 12). Then, the people miraculously crossed the Red/Reed Sea and witnessed the defeat of Pharaoh's army in its churning waters (13:17–14:31). In other words, when the law is given to the nation through Moses, it is directed at a redeemed people. It was not designed to show them *how to achieve redemption*; rather, its purpose was to show them *how to live as a redeemed people*. The account begins with "You yourselves have seen what I did to Egypt, and how I carried you on eagles' wings and brought you to myself" (19:4). The prologue to the Ten Commandments underscores the fact of their redemption: "I am the LORD your God, who brought you out of Egypt, out of the land of slavery" (20:2). The giving of the law then follows this assertion.

The narrative context for the giving of the law can be expanded beyond the preceding chapters in the book of Exodus. In the call of Abram in Genesis 12, the patriarch is told that he and his descendants will be the channel of God's blessing to the rest of the world (12:1–3). Centuries later, when the law is entrusted to Israel, it is presented in such a way so as to communicate that the law itself and the society that it was to shape and regulate are to be a divine blessing. The key text is worth citing in full. Moses is speaking:

> See, I have taught you decrees and laws as the LORD my God commanded me, so that you may follow them in the land you are entering to take possession of it. Observe them carefully, for this will show your wisdom and understanding to the nations, who will hear about all these decrees and say, "Surely this great nation is a wise and understanding people." What other nation is so great as to have their gods near them the way the LORD our God is near us whenever we pray to him? And what other nation is so great as to have such righteous decrees and laws as this body of laws I am setting before you today? (Deut. 4:5–8)

The law and the nations. The content of the law and Israel's adherence to its statutes were designed to point the surrounding peoples to the greatness of God and his wisdom. But there is something more here. Christopher Wright uses the term *paradigm* to explain this other purpose of the law. He explains that these laws "constituted a concrete model, a practical, culturally specific, experimental exemplar of the beliefs and values they embodied."[3] Through the medium of the law and its incarnation in the nation, the moral demands of God would be visible in concrete ways in the multiple spheres of human existence. The law was to offer to the world of that time an example of what a life pleasing to God would look like. One area of the law prescribed to Israel is the attitude toward and treatment of the stranger.

Israel's stance toward the foreigner was part of the larger fabric of its ethical life. It was part of the ethos of what it meant to be the people of God.

The fact that this set of laws was to be a light to the nations does not mean, however, that it would be unique, totally distinct from other ancient Near Eastern law codes. In fact, one should expect some degree of overlap between the laws of the Old Testament and the law collections of other cultures in that geographical area. For one thing, they all deal with conventional social issues, such as marriage, property rights and procedures for inheritance, loans, theft, and murder. Second, it is natural that the broadly shared cultural and historical milieu of Mesopotamia and Syro-Palestine yielded some commonalities in the language and content of these law codes.[4]

At the same time, there are important differences between Israelite law and these other collections. These differences are grounded ultimately in the character of the divine Lawgiver and in what he had done for his people. Recent studies demonstrate the dissimilarities, based on these two foundations, in such areas as the mercy shown to the poor and the political ideology of the monarchy.[5] This will also be apparent in our study of the treatment of the stranger.

One final pertinent observation remains to be made, and it comes from a discipline called interpretive anthropology.[6] Interpretive anthropology teaches us that, although most people do not perceive it in this way, a system of law generates and is a reflection of its culture. In other words, what a particular culture defines as "true" and "right" in terms of legal principles and process is actually its own sociohistorical construct. It has a history; there are reasons why things are the way they are and function as they do. A society's law attempts to put all of life in its proper place and organize its chaos and adjudicate its conflicts. It is, therefore, a window into that society's soul. How the law is structured, the kinds of privileges and protections it offers, the demands and limits it imposes, and the institutions it establishes reveal that society's system of values and priorities. It discloses what that society understands to be correct and good.

This perspective adds another dimension to what we have been saying about Old Testament law. We should recognize that the way it deals with the foreigner says something very important about the heart of Israel and of the God who gave them these rules. Wright is correct that the law was to be a paradigm for the world. Interpretive anthropology would add the insight that it is not just that specific laws serve as a model for other nations. The laws reflect something deeper: Israel's stance toward the foreigner was part of the larger fabric of its ethical life. It was part of the ethos of what it meant to be the people of God.

Terminology for the Sojourner

Nations of the ancient world were not construed as modern nation-states, but there clearly was a sense of having boundaries.

These borders followed, like today, natural geographical or topographical lines (such as rivers and mountains) and could be formalized by treaty. The text is replete with geographical areas connected to different peoples, like the land of Egypt, the Philistines, Moab, Ammon, and Babylon.

Nations could protect their borders with patrols and forts to monitor incursions, peaceful or otherwise. Accordingly, the people of a land distinguished themselves from those who came from somewhere else. They would have come into contact with or seen traders, caravans, mercenaries, political exiles, officials from other nations, fugitives, runaway slaves, refugees, and foreigner settlers. Perhaps they had witnessed other armies marching through their territory. How were outsiders perceived and treated in the ancient Near East?[7] How were these sentiments expressed in law or other legal and social arrangements?

An awareness of boundaries also permeates the Old Testament. For example, Israel is aware that they are crossing into others' territories on their journey to the promised land. They ask permission to pass through but receive a negative response (Num. 20–24; Judg. 11:16–20). This is not surprising. As a large group, Israel would have to eat off the land or secure food from these peoples. Also, these people saw Israel as a military threat, because of what they had heard about the exodus from Egypt.

The promised land is given limits (e.g., Num. 34:1–12; Deut. 11:24). There were many occasions when Israel had disputes about its borders with neighboring nations, such as with the Arameans at Ramoth Gilead (1 Kings 22:1–2; 2 Kings 9:1–5). However, how did Israel react to outsiders who entered into their land? Israel had a long history of having persons of other ethnicities in their midst. For example, Israel left Egypt as a mixed multitude (Exod. 12:38, 48–49); other examples include Moses's Cushite wife (Num. 12:1), Ruth the Moabite, Doeg the Edomite (1 Sam. 21:8), Uriah the Hittite (2 Sam. 11), Zelek the Ammonite and Ittai the Gittite (2 Sam. 15:19–22). In addition,

the Old Testament contains a good amount of legislation dealing with outsiders. Were these laws welcoming and charitable,
or were they exclusionary and punitive?

Several terms are used in the Old Testament to refer to outsiders. They are *gēr*, *tôšab*, *nokrî* (and the related *ben-nēkār*), and
zār.[8] The English versions are not consistent in their translations.
Sometimes the same English word is used for more than one of
these terms and different English words for the same Hebrew
term. Accordingly, in what follows I will stay primarily with the
transliteration of the Hebrew. The next few paragraphs are a
bit technical, but these details can be helpful for our purposes.

Nokrî/ben-nēkār and zār. These words usually convey that
something or someone is non-Israelite.[9] Sometimes this is a neutral, matter-of-fact usage. For instance, when Ruth first speaks
to Boaz, she calls herself a "foreigner" (the feminine form,
nokriyyâ; Ruth 2:10). Solomon uses this term to refer to those
from other countries who would come to worship the Lord at
the temple in Jerusalem (1 Kings 8:41, 43). Often, though, the
idea of foreignness in both these words has a negative connotation. They are used to refer to enemies, strange gods, a licentious
woman, or foreign women of another faith who could corrupt
an Israelite.[10] In these cases, that which is foreign is perceived
as bad or threatening.

The term *nokrî* (and ocasionally *zār*)[11] can refer to foreigners
who dwell in Israel. The profile of the *nokrî* is not altogether
clear. The textual evidence that we have suggests at least two
nuances. To begin with, there is the impression that at least some
of these people have not been in the land very long. David calls
his loyal commander Ittai, a mercenary Gittite, a *nokrî* and then
says, "You came only yesterday" (2 Sam. 15:20). Of course, this
phrase is hyperbole, but it does suggest that Ittai had arrived
recently. This might partly explain Ruth's comment to Boaz,
too; she had not been in Bethlehem very long and probably felt
very out of place.

In other instances, however, it appears that these outsiders did not integrate themselves fully into Israelite life. The law prohibits this kind of foreigner from becoming king (Deut. 17:15) and from participating in some of Israel's rituals (Exod. 12:43; Ezek. 44:7, 9; cf. Lev. 22:25). They could be viewed with suspicion (Ps. 144:7–11). It has been proposed that these may have been foreign merchants or traders, who would have had no reason to commit to the community. It seems that an aspect of their "strangeness" within Israel is that these immigrants may have maintained their own faith and customs (Isa. 2:6; yet 1 Kings 8:41, 43). In Israel, where religion was basic to all of life, this refusal to believe in and follow the Lord was frowned on because of all the implications another religion would have for every sphere of life.

Tôšab. The term *tôšab* is even more difficult to define. It occurs but a few times in the Old Testament. It is almost always found in parallel, either with the "hired worker" (Exod. 12:45; Lev. 22:10; 25:6, 40) or "foreigner" (*gēr*; Lev. 25:23, 35, 47; Num. 35:15).[12] That these persons can be hired hands and that they are listed with the sojourner suggests a couple of things. First, these foreigners (or at least some of them) were economically dependent. There were reasons for this, and we will return to this socioeconomic reality below. Second, there must have been some distinction between the *tôšab* and the sojourner for them to be mentioned together sometimes. They appear with the *nokrî* in the prohibition about the Passover (Exod. 12:43, 45), so maybe they, too, are not as fully assimilated as the *gēr*. We cannot be certain. The scarcity of verses does not allow for any firm conclusions.

Gēr. The term that is most pertinent to this study is *gēr*.[13] It appears especially in the legal material of the Pentateuch, and the next section will explore what those books have to say about these persons. This word has been translated into English as "alien," "resident alien," "stranger," "sojourner," or "foreigner." Interestingly, a new version, the Common English Bible, renders it "immigrant."

Before I move on, though, at least one significant conclusion can be drawn from what has been said thus far. On the basis of their experience and revelation from God, Israel had formulated distinctions between foreigners and made value judgments about them in terms of their integration into the community and their impact on society. The variety in the terminology reflects this.[14] Sadly, the picture offered by word studies is not altogether clear, so tidy definitions are simply not possible.

We probably cannot say much more than distinctions were made based on Israel's interaction with these foreigners. But this is an important point. It is a natural consequence of having others live among a people. Difference is there for all to see. Yet in Israel difference did not remain at the level of observation or lead to sharp separation from all who had found their way to the land. What will prove to be impressive is to see how God calls his people to respond to the *gēr*.

Laws Pertaining to the Sojourner

Ancient Near Eastern law. The first thing that stands out in the study of the sojourner (*gēr*) in Old Testament law is the remarkable contrast that can be drawn with the other law codes of the ancient Near East. In the last chapter it was mentioned that there is evidence from administrative documents about the life of deportees and other foreign individuals and groups in Assyria, Babylon, and Persia. Nevertheless, the law codes are almost totally silent about these people and about those who emigrate from these nations.[15] There are a few laws that deal with the marital and property rights of someone who leaves for a time and returns (Laws of Eshnunna, law 30; Laws of Hammurabi, laws 30, 31, 136).[16] Law 41 of the Laws of Eshnunna refers to a foreigner who it seems is a merchant of some kind, but its interpretation is disputed. Whatever its correct meaning, however, notice the lack of references to the foreigner who had come to live there, no matter the reason and the circumstances. There also are treaties and diplomatic correspondence regarding what to do with runaway slaves and fugitives, but little legislation about those who have moved to dwell in a new land. The legislation in the Old Testament could not be more different.[17] The laws are numerous, and they are gracious to the sojourner. Clearly, Israel had a theological stake in the presence of the outsiders among them. The obvious question is, why? A survey of this legislation will reveal the reasons.

Life as a sojourner. The economy of Israel was agrarian. In the austere environment of that part of the world, life in rural areas could be difficult. In this context, sojourners—those immigrants or refugees who had moved to Israel—were a particularly vulnerable group for two principal reasons. On the one hand, the support of kinship groups was indispensable in times of drought, crop failure, disease, and death. The challenge that sojourners faced when arriving in the land was that they had left behind their kinship network. As a result, they were without the help that only an extended family could offer. Sojourners, therefore, could be particularly vulnerable to the unexpected and sometimes harsh vicissitudes of life. On the other hand, ownership of land was fundamental for making a living and supporting a family in that peasant economy. Inheritance of property went along kinship lines, passing from the father to the appropriate male heir. As foreigners, they were excluded from the land-tenure system.

Without kin and land, many sojourners would be dependent on the Israelites for work, provision, and protection. They could be day laborers (Deut. 24:14), and the Old Testament mentions that they were conscripted to do the hard labor in the building of the temple (1 Chron. 22:2; 2 Chron. 2:17–18). Apparently, a few became successful, but these seem to have been the exception to the rule (Lev. 25:47). Foreigners could be taken advantage of through unfair labor practices, but the law recognized this danger. Sojourners deserved the Sabbath rest from their work like everyone else (Exod. 20:10; Deut. 5:14) and were to receive their wages in a timely manner (Exod. 23:12; Deut. 24:14–15).

The law also recognizes their potentially precarious situation and responds by including them with other sectors of the population who would have been at risk, too: widows and orphans, other hired workers, servants, and the poor.[18] Along with these unfortunates, sojourners qualified for the gleaning law. This stipulated that harvesters leave the edges of a field untouched, so that the needy could gather food (Lev. 19:10; 23:22; Deut. 24:19–22). It is noteworthy that it is while Ruth is working among the harvesters that Boaz spots her (Ruth 2). Sojourners also were to receive a portion of the special tithe that was collected every three years for the poor (Deut. 14:28–29; 26:12–13).

Another natural fear of an outsider pertains to doubts about fair treatment in legal cases. These could involve, for instance, inadequate language skills, lack of knowledge of the law and customs, and the possibility of prejudice by local folk. In response, the law stipulates that sojourners were to receive fair treatment. No predisposition against the foreigner was to be tolerated (Deut. 1:16–17), nor any advantage taken because they were powerless (24:17–18; 27:19).

The prophets thundered against those Israelites who did not accept the responsibility to care for these people. It was a breach of their faith in the Lord, and he would not tolerate this disobedience (Jer. 22:3; Ezek. 22:7, 29; Mal. 3:5; cf. Ps. 94:6). True religion was inseparable from an ethic of charity toward the disadvantaged (Jer. 7:4–8; Zech. 7:8–10).

Motivations behind laws. What was the reason behind these laws and the prophetic tirades? What would have been the motivation to provide for the needs of these outsiders? At least three are outlined in the biblical text.

First, Israel was to be gracious to the outsider because of their history. Life as a sojourner had characterized the experience of the patriarchs (Gen. 23:4; 26:3; Deut. 26:5; the verb *gwr*, Gen. 12:10; 20:1; 21:23, 34; 26:3; etc.). Israel also had been sojourners many years in Egypt. Unfortunately, that long time as an immigrant people had degenerated into a period of oppression. It was to serve as a warning and lesson to not mistreat the sojourners in their midst (Exod. 22:21 [22:20 MT]; 23:9). In fact, God calls Israel sojourners and hired hands in the land (Lev. 25:23). The land ultimately belongs to him, and the Israelites were there only by his grace. The Lord was the owner and patron of that territory, and Israel's task was to work it in obedience to his laws. They were, in essence, his day laborers, and that truth should define how they dealt with those sojourners who lived among them. Sojourning came to be a metaphor, too, of a sense of estrangement from the Lord in times of difficulty (e.g., Ps. 39:12 [MT 39:13]; 119:19; 1 Chron. 29:15).

The command to remember is central to the theology of the book of Deuteronomy, especially as it pertains to the sojourner (5:15; 10:19; 16:12; 24:18, 22; cf. 26:1–11); the warning not to forget the past underscores that imperative (4:9, 23; 6:12; 8:11, 14, 19; 26:13; etc.).[19] Several mechanisms allowed for this memory to be rehearsed periodically and continually in the home, in their communities, and as a nation: the recounting of the historical narrative at several of the feasts, the annual making of booths, and the Sabbath and Passover lessons. The vivid recollection of their past in Egypt under a cruel regime and of that nation's religious system that legitimized that unjust system was to be an important motivator and shaper of the nation's moral life vis-à-vis the vulnerable.

A bit of reflection suggests that these laws, then, were not only to provide for the sojourner in multiple ways; they also were to help the Israelites not to do to others what had happened to them in Egypt. The people of God were not to repeat the ruthless attitudes and actions of the Egyptians. In other words, they were not to become the Egyptians by repeating that cycle of oppression!

Second, the charge to "love your neighbor as yourself" (Lev. 19:18), which Jesus called the second great commandment (Matt. 22:34–40), was extended to the sojourner precisely because of that experience under Pharaoh: "The foreigner residing with you must be treated as your native-born. Love them as yourself, for you were foreigners in Egypt. I am the LORD your God" (Lev. 19:34). The neighbor to be loved was not to be restricted to family members and other native Israelites. The command points to persons beyond those circles, those more difficult to love because of difference. A proper and edifying mind-set, as well as positive actions toward the immigrant, were expected.

The third and the most serious and profound incentive to care for sojourners was to be found in the person of God. In reminding Israel of its history and the obligations that stemmed from it, the Lord explains that the redemption from their horrific experience as immigrants also revealed something very important about his own person: God loves the helpless, among whom he lists the sojourner. Notice that this divine love was concrete, providing food and clothing (Deut. 10:17–18). Israel is to love sojourners, because God does (Deut. 10:19; cf. Ps. 146:6–9), and, of course, they would be the means by which that food and clothing would reach the sojourner. Consequently, to ignore this call of God and the cry of the sojourner would be a sin (Deut. 24:14–15).

In sum, ancient Israel did not have the kind of government programs and social systems in place that we have today, which provide assistance through local, state, and federal programs. Help for the needy had to occur at several levels and through various channels: individual families (giving rest on the Sabbath, including sojourners in celebrations), the community (gleaning laws), workplaces of whatever kind (payment of wages, periodic rest), religious centers (collecting of the tithe), and at the city gate with the elders or other legal gatherings (fairness in legal matters). Everyone in a sense was involved somehow in the care of the sojourner. The prophets make clear that God held everyone responsible, from individuals to society as a whole.

Integration of the sojourner. In the law we see that Israel opened the most central—and most precious—sphere of its life to sojourners: its religion. This faith was foundational to its identity as a people and marked Israel as different from the surrounding nations. It permeated daily, weekly, monthly, and annual activities and shaped every aspect of its existence. And into this world the sojourner was given entry. Sojourners were permitted to participate in the Sabbath (Exod. 20:10; Deut. 5:14), the Day of Atonement (Lev. 16:29–30), the Passover (Exod. 12:48–49; Num. 9:14), the Feast of Weeks (Deut. 16:11), the Feast of Tabernacles (Deut. 16:14), and Firstfruits (Deut. 26:11). Forgiveness for unintentional sin was extended to them (Num. 15:27–29), and they were afforded access to the cities of refuge (Num. 35:15). Tellingly, the sojourner is listed with the rest of the people in the covenant renewal ceremony of Deuteronomy 29 (vv. 9–15).

Expectations and responsibilities were placed on sojourners as well. They were to be present at the periodic reading of the law (Deut. 31:10–13). This makes sense. It would be in listening to the law that sojourners could learn more about what it meant to be a member of that society. Listening together with the rest of the people at the Feast of Tabernacles would be a public demonstration of their solidarity with Israel and, in turn, Israel's acceptance of them. This scene also assumes that sojourners spoke and understood Hebrew so that they could follow the reading. The language would also be a prerequisite to participating in the other religious and civic activities.

Sojourners were subject to the penalties of criminal laws (Lev. 24:22), many of the dietary restrictions (Exod. 12:19; Lev.

17:10–15), the sexual taboos (Lev. 18:26), purity laws (Num. 19:10), the regulations for the feasts (Num. 9:14; 15:15), and the prohibition against the worship of other gods and blasphemy against the Lord (Lev. 20:1–2; 24:10–16; Num. 15:30–31). A number of these regulations and several of those cited in the preceding paragraph contain the phrase "whether he is a native-born Israelite or a foreigner." This expresses in another way

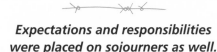

Expectations and responsibilities were placed on sojourners as well.

their equal standing before the law.[20] In the worldview of ancient Israel, the sojourner should not contribute to the polluting of the land by violating these laws, which would result in judgment (Lev. 17:8–9; 18:24–30).

Still, some distinctions were made between the native Israelite and the sojourner. For example, there were dietary laws that did not apply to sojourners (Deut. 14:21). There was also reluctance to be charitable to certain foreigners and allow them to participate in civic gatherings (Deut. 23:3–8 [MT 23:4–9]), but there are occasions when this rule was ignored or superseded. Ruth is the stellar example of this, and Solomon's prayer of dedication counters it as well (1 Kings 8:41–43).[21]

Future hope. Finally, there is the prophetic hope that one day the connection between sojourner and native Israelite would be closer. Ezekiel 47:21–23 envisions a time when sojourners will be able to inherit land along with the tribes of Israel. The barrier against possessing their own parcels of the promised land would be done away with. When Isaiah talks of the future ingathering of Israel from exile and depicts their coming to worship at Zion, the holy mountain of God, he includes the "foreigner" (56:1–8; cf. 2:2–4; 14:1). Interestingly, he uses the term *nokrî*, not *gēr*.[22] These are people from other lands who will come before the Lord, echoing that hope of Solomon in 1 Kings 8:41–43. Foreigner and Israelite together will enjoy his presence in glorious fashion. The breadth of God's mercy and the response of the peoples of the world to his person will not be limited to the native-born or to the boundaries of Israel.

The uniqueness of Israel's laws for the sojourner. We began this section saying that Israel's law was unique in its treatment of the outsider, both in the number of laws and in their generosity. Unlike some have argued, these laws make no distinction between "legal" and "illegal" immigrants."[23] Nothing in the laws suggests this distinction that has dominated the current debate. Could there have been some sort of legal means to secure entry and residency in ancient Israel? Perhaps, but nothing along this vein appears in the biblical text. Was there a formal monitoring of the flow of persons across Israel's borders? Again, nothing of the sort is mentioned. Instead, the text suggests a surprising openness for the ancient world.

This review of these laws, especially with regard to their motivations, provides an answer to the question of why they are different from the law codes of the surrounding peoples. It is because of Israel's special story and the character of the Lord that they were to treat the sojourner in such a caring manner. Their concern for the vulnerable from another land was fundamental to their witness and life as the people of God.

Implications for Today

Different concepts of law. This cursory survey of Old Testament legislation dealing with the sojourner can be instructive in several ways. First of all, the short discussion on law and culture that is informed by cultural anthropology is pertinent. Because Hispanics come from another culture, their concept of law will differ from the way it is understood in this country.

My life has been spent straddling North American Anglo and Latin American cultures. One major difference between these two cultures, to which anyone who has traveled or lived south of the border can attest, is the different appreciation of the meaning and practice of law. This can be empirically verified by anyone at a personal level simply, for instance, by trying to obtain a driver's license, get a visa, pay a fine, conduct a bank transaction, or get a package from a customs house. It quickly becomes apparent that law and laws are inseparable from bureaucratic protocol and artificial (but very important!) formalities, social status, and family connections.

These attitudes and the nature of laws can be traced to a cultural history quite distinct from that of the United States. Latin American law finds its origins on the Iberian Peninsula, not in a British heritage. The different branches of government also identify their function and rights in ways that are different from this country, and each branch as well must define itself in relationship to the military establishment (although this has been changing during the past several decades). These and other factors yield a very dissimilar legal culture, which impacts politics and the world of business and their corresponding legal values and structures. In Latin America, all of this is normal and natural; it is the way things have always been, and change comes slowly. Latin America would not be Latin America without this particular flavor of the spice of life. The majority culture in the US should anticipate that the adaptation by immigrants to the laws and legal ethos of the United States will take time. Hispanic immigrants, too, will need to listen to and acquaint themselves with the law of the land (cf. Deut. 31:10–13).

Varied experiences. Second, the Old Testament presents a realistic picture of an ancient society trying to come to grips with a complex social issue. Several terms are applied to outsiders. Even though it is hard to make definitive comments about their meanings, the fact that there were multiple labels for foreigners in Israel suggests that the experiences with outsiders were varied and that these individuals could be evaluated in different ways. This pattern also is true now of the assessment by the majority culture of other people who have come from a Hispanic culture. In other words, a variety of reactions to the arrival and presence of Hispanic immigrants, today's sojourners, is to be expected.

Law as paradigm. A third point is based on Wright's thesis that the law of Israel is to serve as a paradigm for other nations. It is to be a live illustration of the ethical orientation for life that God intends for all humanity. The next component of this model, which was not mentioned earlier, is Wright's contention that the moral values of Israel's law that found expression in specific regulations relevant to that ancient context are pertinent to the modern era, too. Deuteronomy 4:5–8 points beyond its particular setting. The law was to be an object lesson to the surrounding nations then and now. Obviously, the structures, institutions, and other initiatives corresponding to those same values today will look different than they did millennia ago. But God's enduring ethical ideals continue to be valid and should be made concrete in the contemporary world.

Care for the sojourner is one of those ideals. It was a moral demand that set God's people apart from the other nations; even more significantly, it was grounded in God's person. Not to be hospitable, individually or collectively, merited the wrath of the prophets. The law reflects an awareness that sojourners were vulnerable, and so in it are found a series of mechanisms to help meet their physical needs. To this charitable socioeconomic framework is added an invitation to the sojourner into what made Israel, Israel: its religious life.

If what Wright proposes is correct, and I believe it is, then the imperative of caring for the sojourner is also binding today on every nation. At the very least, this ethical commitment should resonate especially with the people of God in the majority culture. It ought to be demonstrated in specific measures that respond to the needs of the immigrant. The means will vary according to the opportunities and limitations in any given context, but the responsibility remains. It also will entail majority-culture Christians and churches opening themselves up and allowing the sojourner admittance to their culture and lives. In addition, if this moral imperative is for all nations, then these Christians have the obligation to be a voice for God's heart for the sojourner in the country at large. Again, the Bible does not provide a blueprint for action, but it does make its call clear.

Identity. In addition to the reality of varied responses and the moral imperative, there is yet another lesson to be learned. Care for the sojourner was important for Israel because they, too, had experienced life as sojourners—and that in most unpleasant ways. The rehearsing at the feasts of their history as immigrants in Egypt and the reminder to be gracious to outsiders and the downcast were exercises in collective memory. All of this, ideally, was crucial for their formation as a people of virtue, especially the virtue of generous hospitality. Stated another way, the arrival and presence of sojourners were *not a threat to Israel's national identity*; rather, their presence was *fundamental to its very meaning*. The people of Israel could not be who they were supposed to be before God and the world if they forgot who they had been and from where they had come. Note, too, that concern for sojourners was part of an expansive ethical vision for the needy that included widows, orphans, and the poor. In the biblical view, one cannot isolate vulnerable groups that one does not want to engage from the comprehensive biblical call to incarnate God's presence and care for all in need.

While the text is speaking about the people of God, there may be an analogy with the United States. Today some deny that this country should be understood as a nation of immigrants. It is said that there have always been restrictions and preferential quotas and that the country has been ambivalent toward those from other lands. This is true, but what this position cannot deny is that every year for over two centuries there has been a flow of immigrants—with or without quotas, with permission or without proper documents—arriving on these shores. The numbers may vary, the color of the faces might change, but the reality of continual immigration is a fact. Immigration is inseparable from the history of the nation and is fundamental to its identity.

Every family can point back to parents or grandparents or great-grandparents who came from somewhere else. It is part of our familial memory, but at the national level there is collective amnesia. What we celebrate are vestiges of immigrant memories that are often reduced to a parade and food and drink (St. Patrick's Day, Oktoberfest, Columbus Day). What has been forgotten are the prejudices and the marginalization of those earlier immigrants, the ghettoes and the exploitation of their labor. To deny the hard and unpleasant parts of the past in order to control the present and to shape the future as we would like might be a greater threat to national identity.

Laws, especially as they pertain to the vulnerable (widows, orphans, the poor, the physically and mentally challenged, and the immigrant), can be a window into a country's soul. What do they say about us and the breadth and depth of our compassion? Ideally, those measures designed to organize and appropriately deal with immigration and immigrants should reflect the virtues of kindness, generosity, and patience instead of being motivated by fear or prejudice.

Broad responsibility. As mentioned previously, it is interesting to observe that the responsibility to take care of the sojourner in Israel was carried out at many levels, through families, religious centers, and other local initiatives. This was necessitated because of the nature of the ancient context. The modern world is different. Still, while today the government usually is expected to handle such matters, there may be some value in a more multipronged approach that is more inclusive.

Wider participation yields deeper social awareness and ethical concern.

Multiple reactions. At least two final lessons are directed more specifically at the immigrant. To begin with, the evidence provided by our discussion on the terminology used to refer to foreigners in the Old Testament should lead these sojourners to anticipate diverse reactions to their coming here. Sometimes those who are native-born will qualify foreignness in a neutral fashion, simply as a label; on other occasions foreignness will be considered something negative (and in a few cases this might be deserved). In the greater number of instances, however, immigrants may experience the welcome of the majority culture. In their labors, they may benefit, too, from the generosity of individuals of the majority culture and the "safety net" afforded by this country's legislation (such as schooling for children and emergency-room care) and myriad independent organizations and Christian ministries. The problem is that the United States does not have a law revealed from heaven, and so the legal system is imperfect and is now being contested and reworked. So there are times when the laws will be of assistance and other times when they could be contradictory, unreasonable, and unjust. As the process of immigration reform moves forward, much will depend on the heart of the majority culture, but there is also a responsibility that the sojourner must accept. This is the second point.

Cultural accommodation. Second, the Old Testament law makes clear that there were expectations for the sojourner, just as there were demands on Israel. Some of the Christian literature that champions the immigrant draws from the law only a few verses that command the care of the sojourner. This could be a strategic decision to convince audiences of the need to provide for the needy immigrant, and I can appreciate that. But ultimately, such an approach is one-sided and incomplete. The law assumes that there is movement on the part of the sojourner toward the host culture (Israel): learning its ways and its language and respecting its laws and taboos. There are cases of exemplary foreigners who moved to and lived within Israel.

What we will never know is to what extent these individuals accommodated themselves to the culture of Israel and how much of their home culture they retained; most assuredly, it differed for each one. Countless Hispanics are trying to learn the ways of the United States, do appreciate the importance of learning English, and want to be respectful of US customs. I have heard this commitment from Hispanic pastors, who are counseling their people toward these ends. I have seen it in many persons who are trying to better their lives here and raise their children in constructive ways. Adaptation is occurring, but how much of home will be retained will depend on a variety of factors relative to each person, family, and community.

Conclusion

Whereas the preceding chapter on the Old Testament high-lighted the theme of the image of God and then demonstrated how ubiquitous experiences of living in other countries are in the biblical text, this chapter began with hospitality and then explored the laws regarding the sojourner. Other issues in the Old Testament could be relevant to the immigration debate, but I end my reflections here.

The goal has been to try to uncover a biblical point of view—or, perhaps better, a more biblically grounded attitude—toward immigrants and immigration. It is a topic close to the heart of God and inseparable from the life and mission of God's people. Openness to outsiders is a virtue, and concern for their well-being is manifested tangibly in Old Testament law. For their part, foreigners were to respond in positive ways to this invitation to enter the world of Israel.

These truths should help orient how majority-culture and Hispanic Christians wrestle with the immigration quandary. With hearts attuned to the will of God, perhaps the tenor of the debate can be leavened with grace and any proposed solutions and compromises guided by divine wisdom. The next chapter will complement what has been presented thus far with the contribution of the New Testament.

4

Welcoming the Stranger

Guidance from the New Testament

Today Jesus comes in many shapes and colors. One has only to enter "images of Jesus" in Google's search engine and click. Instantly, hundreds of different portrayals of Jesus are available. He appears as Caucasian, African American, Caribbean, Asian, black African, and some sort of Hispanic; he can be meek or manly, pious or warlike, an Eastern Orthodox mystic or a Che Guevara look-alike, a beggar or an entrepreneur who can give guidance to modern CEOs. The possibilities are as varied as the human imagination. Jesus takes on the form of the beholder, amenable to the beholder's own view of life but often missing important dimensions of the portrait of Jesus in the New Testament.

This tendency is true as well in academic circles. In the past thirty years or so, numerous publications have argued that the historical Jesus was not the divine Son of God of Christian orthodoxy but instead, for example, a peasant cynic or a mystic.

The global response to *The Da Vinci Code* and the spectacular claims associated with the *Gospel of Judas* or other apocryphal gospels are evidence of the power that Jesus holds over the general public, but also of how fascinated people are with alternative views that reduce Jesus to the merely human. During this same time period more circumspect scholarship has been focusing anew on the Jewish backgrounds of Jesus and the trustworthiness of the Gospel accounts.[1]

This more confident orientation is helpful as we go to the Gospels for insights into the Hispanic immigration debate. How so? What Jesus said and did is real and, if one claims to be a follower of Jesus, these things matter. A better sense of the sociocultural context of his time can also help us better understand any ethical demands he might have made that still have a claim on Christians.

Having said this, though, a reading of the four Gospels makes it clear that Jesus never dealt directly with the topic of immigration per se. At the same time, however, Jesus did give attention to others who were not Jews or who were marginalized and deemed less valuable as persons (such as women and lepers). If the good news was for all humankind, then Jesus had to expand his disciples' vision to embrace all kinds of people. For his followers and others who heard him, cultural identity was a fundamental issue. If the immigration discussion concerns cultural identity—and it clearly does—then it is important for Christians to see how Jesus dealt with those who were different and to learn from his teaching on such things.

This chapter, therefore, begins with a look at material in the Gospels. I will highlight two of the experiences of Jesus and then discuss two passages of his teaching that are pertinent to our topic. The second section turns to the First Epistle of Peter, which utilizes the language of sojourner in reference to the church. The third section returns to the theme of hospitality that we looked at in chapter 3. The fourth and last section briefly examines Romans 13. This passage brings up the question of legality. Undocumented immigrants have violated laws of the United States, and that inescapable fact, it is said, should be the basis of any treatment of issues concerning immigration. I have left discussion of Romans 13 until last for a reason. It is the place to end our survey, not the place to begin the conversation.

Learning from Jesus

Jesus the Refugee

Not long after Jesus was born, he and his parents had to leave Bethlehem. The Gospel of Matthew informs us that Herod the Great wanted to kill him (Matt. 2:13–14). Herod had been told by the magi that they were on their way to see the newborn king of the Jews (2:1–8). Herod was fearful and jealous of any rival to his throne. When the magi did not report back, Herod ordered the slaughter of all the young boys in the area around Bethlehem (2:16–18). This characterization of Herod as paranoid and ruthless fits other portrayals of the king from that period.[2]

Joseph, Mary, and the child Jesus sought asylum in Egypt. There was a large Jewish population in Egypt, especially in Alexandria, so it was natural that they go there. They left in haste after the angel's warning and probably took few possessions with them in order to be able to travel quickly and avoid Herod's troops. There are no details of this sojourn in Egypt, and Matthew is the only Gospel that records it. Apparently, the stay in Egypt was short, perhaps no more than two years. An angel informed the family that Herod had died (2:19–21; 4 BC). They first had wanted to go to their ancestral town, Bethlehem, but Herod's son Archelaus was reigning now over Judea. His reputation for cruelty was reminiscent of his father's (2:22), so Joseph took the family northward and returned once more to Nazareth in Galilee.

The joy of the nativity scene and the wonder of the visit of the magi are overshadowed by the unhappy account of the senseless death of innocent children and the flight of refugees. The migration of this family locates the Jesus story within a movement that spans history, of people desiring a better life or escaping the threat of death.

Jesus and Outsiders

The setting. First-century Palestine was a complicated place.[3] Geographically, it was divided into six principal regions. On the west side of the Dead Sea, the Jordan River, and the Sea of Galilee, from south to north, were Idumea, Judea, Samaria, and Galilee; across the Jordan were Perea and the Decapolis. Politics was a knotty state of affairs. The area was under the overall rule of the Roman Empire, but there was considerable autonomy. Depending on local circumstances and history, the empire appointed regional governors or permitted others, such as Herod the Great, to rule limited kingdoms. In return, Rome expected them to collect taxes, keep the peace, and maintain loyalty to Caesar. Palestine was volatile, with strong political rivalries and a vocal population unafraid to appeal to Rome to express their discontent.

The religious world also was very complex. The gods of Greco-Roman religion, the mystery cults, and emperor worship all had their adherents. Divisions within the Jewish faith added yet more color and confusion to the religious landscape. Among the Jews in Judea were several sects, the most significant being the Pharisees, Sadducees, and Essenes. Although the Pharisees were the most influential group in terms of setting the agenda for religious practices, apparently much of the populace did not align itself formally with any one of these groups. Under Herod, Jerusalem had become a world-class city, and pilgrims from all over came to worship at the temple and participate in the Jewish festivals.

Within the region of Samaria resided the Samaritans.[4] They practiced a form of Judaism, but they had a different holy mountain (Mount Gerizim), their own priesthood, and special beliefs and rituals. They were not accepted as equals by other Jews, and the antipathy between them ran deep. Samaritans were despised because to the Jews they represented a perversion of the faith of Abraham, Isaac, and Jacob. Over the course of centuries the antagonism was marked by a series of betrayals and acts of revenge. In 128 BC the Jewish leader Hyrcanus took over Samaria and burned down the Samaritan sanctuary on Mount Gerizim; in 107 BC he destroyed Shechem. In AD 6/7, during Jesus's youth, Samaritans infiltrated the Passover celebration in Jerusalem and scattered bones in the temple, thereby defiling it. Other incidents date after the time of Jesus and confirm the ongoing animosity. For example, in AD 52, the Samaritans slaughtered a company of pilgrims from Galilee who were on their way to Jerusalem for Passover. This atrocity degenerated into a spiral of violence that led to several interventions by the Romans.

The Samaritans were loathed by the Jews. This hostility is the background for the ministry of Jesus to Samaritans and his appeal to them in his teaching. To do anything charitable for a Samaritan or to say something favorable about them would have been met with dismay by his followers. The disciples' dislike of the Samaritans is illustrated by their reaction to a Samaritan village's rejection of Jesus (Luke 9:51–56). James and John, the "sons of thunder" (Mark 3:17), wanted to call down fire from heaven, perhaps as Elijah had done so many years before (1 Kings 18; 2 Kings 1). To the Jews, the Samaritans were not only religious outsiders; they were enemies. But Jesus would have none of it and rebuked the disciples.

Jesus's personal encounters. The best-known story of Jesus engaging Samaritans is found in the Gospel of John, chapter 4—the account of his conversation with the woman at Jacob's well. This chapter is often cited in discussions about cross-cultural missions, and that can be a suitable appropriation or application of the account.[5] I would like to concentrate, however, more particularly on the significance of Jesus, a rabbi, speaking with a Samaritan, and more specifically, a Samaritan woman. In Jewish tradition Samaritan women were considered to be always unclean; they were categorized as menstruants from the cradle.[6] That this woman is of questionable repute (John 4:16–18) makes Jesus's dialogue with her even more impressive. The extraordinariness of what he does is recognized by the woman herself ("You are a Jew and I am a Samaritan woman. How can you ask me for a drink?") and is emphasized by the text's side comment, "For Jews do not associate with Samaritans" (4:9).

At this point in the narrative Jesus is traveling from Judea to Galilee with his disciples. Of course, geographically Samaria lay between the two. It is commonly said that Jesus chose not to take the circuitous route along the eastern side of the Jordan River, which Jews would follow to avoid ritual contamination and confrontation with Samaritans, so that he could have this encounter. Though the decision to take the longer route may have been made by some Jews, other sources tell us that many preferred the shorter, more direct way, even though the trip through Samaria might not be pleasant.[7]

The text says, "Now he *had* to go through Samaria" (4:4, emphasis added). The English "he had" is the translation of the Greek *dei*, an impersonal verb. A literal rendering of the line would be, "Now *it was necessary* for him to go through Samaria" (the same verb appears earlier in 3:7, 14, 30). This was the road required to journey north, but another level of necessity is at work. This occasion was an important part of what Jesus needed to do for his mission. This meeting is not an unplanned, coincidental happenstance. It is part of the predetermined plan of Jesus.

His disciples had gone ahead to buy food, but Jesus sits at the well and waits. The woman arrives alone to draw water.

Normally, women would go in groups to do this work. Later we learn that she has not been chaste, so perhaps she would go alone out of shame or because she was shunned by other women. Jesus asks her to serve him some water. This Jewish rabbi was asking a Samaritan woman for help! This was remarkable in its countercultural effect. If he were to drink water from a vessel given to him by this woman, Jesus would render himself ritually impure. Jesus, however, does not hesitate. In the give-and-take of their exchange, Jesus leads the woman to consider divine living water (4:10–15) and true worship (4:19–24), and at the end Jesus reveals that he is Messiah (4:25–26). Although it is impossible to know what the woman actually understood about Jesus at this point, she runs to bring others to hear him (4:28–30), and many do believe (4:39–42). Those who respond are concrete evidence that the harvest indeed is at hand (4:34–38)—and it is beginning with Samaritans . . . in Samaria!

Another incident with a Samaritan is found in the Gospel of Luke, chapter 17. Jesus is close to Samaria, verse 11 says, so we do not know if the village he enters was located in Samaria or Galilee. Since Jesus is headed south to Jerusalem, it could very well have been in Samaria. There he hears ten lepers calling out to him (Luke 17:11–13). They stand at a distance, because, according to Jewish purity laws, their disease made them unclean (Lev. 13:45–46; Num. 5:2–3). Jesus tells them to go present themselves to the priests, as stipulated in the law for those who have been cured (Lev. 13:19; 14:1–11). And so it happens: they are cured on their journey. Only one of the ten, though, returns to thank him with wonderful humility and gratitude, throwing himself at Jesus's feet in praise to God.

The text then provides information that it has held back until this moment: "and he was a Samaritan" (Luke 17:16). Once more the faith of a Samaritan is exemplary. Jesus underscores the incongruity of being embraced by a Samaritan. He is on his way to the Holy City to be rejected by the Jews, but "this foreigner" believes (17:18). It is possible that Jesus's parting words to the man mean that he alone of the ten achieved full reconciliation with God (17:19).[8]

In both encounters these Samaritan individuals are doubly outcast. To begin with, both are Samaritans. What is more, the first was morally suspect, the second a leper. Jesus transcends the long-standing enmity between the Jews and Samaritans. He accepts the "other," and they accept him. In all of this, Jesus never ceases to be a Jew. Yet he is able to integrate his cultural

Jesus models a new and different way of looking at persons who are outside the circle of the known and beyond acceptability.

core with other transcendent commitments and gracious attitudes that move him beyond the closed society of his peers.

Jesus's teaching. The teaching of Jesus, like his actions, is designed in part to push the boundaries of the understanding of his followers. Jesus models a new and different way of looking at persons who are outside the circle of the known and beyond acceptability. He displays this in the way he treats those who are in some sense the marginalized of society (women, the poor, the sick) and those who are outsiders (gentiles and Samaritans). What he teaches reinforces and explains that commitment. Two passages are especially relevant. The first deals with a Samaritan, while the second mentions the "stranger" in the context of the final judgment.

Throughout his ministry Jesus had exchanges with religious leaders. Some had sincere motives and wanted to comprehend God better; others probed Jesus for less noble reasons, trying to trick him into making self-incriminating statements.

The latter appears to be the case in the Gospel of Luke, chapter 10. A scribe ("an expert in the law") rises and confronts Jesus with a question about eternal life (Luke 10:25). Jesus responds with another question that challenges the scribe: "What is written in the law? . . . How do you read it?" (10:26). The scribe answers by saying that one must follow the command to love God (Deut. 6:5) and neighbor (Lev. 19:18). Jesus agrees and commands that he obey those injunctions (Luke 10:27–28).

Something in Jesus's response or tone, however, spurred the scribe to ask a follow-up question: "And who is my neighbor?" He is soliciting a definition as to whom he, as a Jew, should love (10:29). Within that context, the scribe may have been wondering if the neighbor should be limited to his own religious circle or could include any member of the Jewish community. Jesus replies with what is now called the parable of the good Samaritan (10:30–37).[9]

In this parable, a priest and a Levite pass by a man who has been attacked by robbers. The scene and description were very realistic for those days, so the story would have immediately captured the audience's attention. No motive is given for why the religious leaders avoid the injured man, but it can be assumed that they fear contamination by one who may be dead (10:30). After they depart from the scene, the anticipation would have been that the next person in the story be a common lay Jew, who would demonstrate a purer, simpler faith. Instead, surprisingly, that person is a Samaritan. The Samaritan not only stops to treat the wounds of the man, but he also takes him to an inn, cares for the man there, and then promises to pay for anything that might be needed in his absence.

The question that had been posed to Jesus was, "Who is my neighbor?" The parable complicates what the scribe expected to hear. Whereas the original issue concerned identifying the neighbor the scribe should love, Jesus leaves no doubt in the parable that it is the neighbor who loves, and he loves in very tangible ways. That neighbor, though, is a Samaritan, an enemy and scorned one; *this* is the neighbor who loves! The Samaritan, not the religious leaders (of whom the scribe was one), sets the example. Jesus forces the scribe to acknowledge this truth by asking the obvious question, "Which of these three do you think was a neighbor . . . ?" The scribe responds correctly, but he cannot bring himself to say "the Samaritan." The benevolent person is simply called "the one who had mercy on him" (10:36).

Jesus concludes their exchange by telling the scribe to emulate that neighbor, the Samaritan, in order to fulfill the command to love (10:37). Once again, the people of God are taught about true faith through an encounter with one outside of and rejected by their culture.

The second passage is the discourse of Matthew 25:31–46. This is part of the longer exchange between Jesus and his disciples on the Mount of Olives not too long before the crucifixion (24:1–25:46). In these verses Jesus speaks about the final judgment of the nations of the world. This passage draws on imagery from the Old Testament and other Jewish literature.[10] In those texts God usually functions as the judge, but there are cases where judgment is performed by another end-time figure he appoints. Here that individual is the Son of Man, who acts in the name of his Father. The divine decision regarding merited eternal blessing and eternal judgment is based on how people have treated the Son of Man/King and the "least of these brothers and sisters of mine" (25:40).

These verses are relevant to the immigration discussion because of the use of the word *stranger* (or *foreigner*, Greek *xenos*) in Matthew 25:35, 38, 43, and 44. This term is included with the hungry, thirsty, naked, sick, and imprisoned, and all of these are called the "least of these brothers and sisters of mine" (25:40, 45). Some believe that this listing of those who suffer, along with the stranger, shows the breadth of Jesus's concern for the needy and emphasizes the ethical demand placed on all humankind. To ignore any of these people, these "little ones," is tantamount to refusing Jesus himself.[11] Since the stranger is one of them, here we have the moral imperative to take care of the immigrant.

At first glance, this interpretation is attractive, but it is not as obvious as it might appear at first glance. In the Gospel of Matthew "little ones" refers to the disciples of Jesus (10:42; 18:6, 10, 14), as do his "brothers and sisters" (except when the reference is to earthly siblings).[12] This passage, therefore, could very well speak of the hardships of disciples, the messengers of the gospel, and their treatment by the nations.[13] The theme of their reception as they go out in Jesus's name appeared earlier in the ministry of the Twelve (10:11–42). To scorn the disciples and their message is to reject Jesus, the one who is the essence of that message and who sends the disciples. Their future itinerant ministry would make them "strangers" wherever they go. Accordingly, within the trajectory of the book, Matthew 25:31–46 sets the stage for the commission to go to all the world in 28:16–20. In his epistles, Paul makes frequent mention of the many hardships in his travels, and the apostle publicly commends those who receive him graciously (e.g., 1 Cor. 16:5–9; Gal. 4:13–14; cf. 3 John 5–10) and encourages others to do the same (e.g., Rom. 16:1–2; 1 Cor. 16:10–12).

Implications for Today

No direct teaching. This brief survey confirms that there is no explicit teaching on immigration in the Gospels. What this does *not* mean, however, is that there is nothing relevant to the immigration discussion.

To begin with, one of the few incidents mentioned about the childhood of Jesus is that he and his family were refugees. They flee to another country for safety. This account, as we saw with other migration stories in the Old Testament, provides those who have had to emigrate from their homeland a point of special connection to the text. Aspects of their own situation and experiences are analogous to the details of this story of Jesus.[14] Sometimes those who have been able to live stable lives and pursue careers and raise their families in peace and comfort in one place may not be able to sense the power of this account of Jesus in the same way.

The "stranger" and the separation of the sheep and goats at the final judgment may not apply directly to the topic of immigration, but at second glance an important admonition could be suggested there. In chapter 1 it was pointed out that within the Hispanic community—those who have been here for generations as well as more recent immigrants, whether documented or undocumented—are many millions of Christians. In the Matthew passage the "stranger" is technically a disciple who goes to another land for ministry and thus is a foreigner there. I do not make a one-to-one correspondence between the disciples of Matthew 25 and all Hispanic immigrants, but it does seem to me that the care of disciples Jesus demands is pertinent to some extent. Many Hispanic believers who come as immigrants are needy. Does not the Christian church of the host culture have some responsibility to help "the least of these" in the name of Jesus? Does not Christ dwell among and in them, too? Would this revelation that the judgment on the nations is based in part on the treatment of disciples have any application to the United States? Will the Son of Man and the Father in any way demand an accounting of this country's actions toward Christian Hispanic immigrants?[15]

Encountering the outsider. There is much to be gleaned for immigration discussions from the way Jesus deals with Samaritans, both in his personal ministry and in his teaching. The Samaritans were culturally different from the Jews; they were despised and discriminated against. Jesus turns these attitudes on their heads by having direct contact with Samaritans (one a woman and the other a leper) and using a Samaritan in a parable. In these passages, Samaritans are models of genuine relationship with God. Jesus does and says these things as a member of the majority culture of his time.

A key issue today concerns how the majority culture in the US perceives national cultural identity and its maintenance in light of the growing presence of Hispanics. This is a natural concern, even though, as we explained in the first chapter, it is more complicated than many think. The point here is that Jesus confronts the identity question head-on through what he does with Samaritans. Even as he continues to live as a Jew, Jesus lays aside his culture's exclusivistic mores and negative feelings toward Samaritans for more important things: their value as persons and the potential of their faith. Jesus gives worth, hope, and direction to a woman who has had a rough life; he heals a leper and brings him joy and a future.

Jesus's actions and attitudes transcend cultural identity; they also help define what it means to be his follower. To stress this is not to deny the many contributions of culture or the importance of a specific identity, but it does put these concerns into perspective. Perhaps these things have to be held a bit more loosely so that we can have the freedom to engage those from other backgrounds and cultures. Of course, these same comments are directed at Hispanics and Hispanic culture(s), too. Hispanics also are wrestling with cultural maintenance and change. This was a topic in chapter 1. All of us must learn from Jesus.

The bigger picture. Jesus's treatment of the Samaritans is but one piece of his proactive consideration of those who were marginalized in his society.[16] It is one dimension of a larger set of ethical commitments. He reaches out to the poor, the sick, women, sinners of all kinds, gentiles, and Samaritans. In light of this truth, a fundamental question must be asked. Does what Jesus did and said have any relevance for Christians today? Is he simply our Savior, one to whom we turn in faith for eternal redemption? Or, in addition to our personal salvation, is his life a model for all time of how to live a life that pleases God and reflects his character on earth? In a sense, we are returning to the dialogue between the Jewish scribe and Jesus. What does God require of those who claim to be believers?

If the life and words of Jesus in some fashion are important and binding on Christians, then other questions follow. Do we, as Christians, have as comprehensive an ethic as Jesus had? If not, why not? What areas of life have been left out? Have attitudes and actions toward immigrants been integrated into that

Jesus's actions and attitudes transcend cultural identity; they also help define what it means to be his follower.

ethic? Along with what are normally highlighted as Christian duties, such as honesty in the workplace, fidelity in marriage, and good stewardship of money, must also stand compassion toward the outsider.

These next two sections are briefer than this one on the Gospels. Each in some way builds off discussions from previous chapters. The first section below looks at the use of sojourner vocabulary in the First Epistle of Peter, and the one that follows revisits the theme of hospitality.

Christians as Sojourners

1 Peter

The terminology of the sojourner appears several times in the First Epistle of Peter.[17] The recipients of the letter are called strangers (*parepidēmos*) in 1:1, and foreigners and strangers (*paroikos* and *parepidēmos*) in 2:11. In the Greco-Roman world these words referred to outsiders who had moved into an area to reside there, perhaps by force or of their own volition. A "stranger" was a more transient resident than was the "foreigner." These outsiders were not granted the rights and privileges of full citizenship, and so they had to endure economic, political, and social limitations. Because they were different, they were not always welcome in their new home. Some commentators understand these labels to refer at some level to the sociopolitical status of the believers who received this letter. Their conversion to the Christian faith would have added to their foreignness in that context.

Commentators apply these terms, by extension, to all Christians. Based on other New Testament texts, it is argued that believers have their ultimate citizenship in heaven. We are foreigners in this fallen world, who are journeying on to our celestial home (cf. Phil. 3:20; Heb. 13:14). Another spiritual nuance points to the apostle Paul's application of this vocabulary to gentile Christians. In the past they were separated from the people of God but are now brought into the household of faith through faith in Christ (Eph. 2:19). In both cases, the New Testament teaches that all Christians are foreigners and strangers because of their distinct set of commitments and values vis-à-vis the society in which we live.

The combination "foreigners and strangers" in 2:11 appears in a very significant place in the Septuagint (i.e., the Greek Old Testament): Genesis 23:4. This is the passage where Abraham buys land from Ephron the Hittite to bury his wife Sarah. This Old Testament allusion connects the experience of the addressees of this letter (and all believers) back to the ancient patriarch. Their sojourning is not unique. The history of the people of God is the pilgrimage of faith of those who are alienated from the world. Abraham's sojourning was literal and spiritual. He was an outsider without land or roots in the region in which he had settled, and he followed another god.

Whether these Christians were sojourners in the Greco-Roman sense or whether the language is simply a way of describing the discrimination suffered by believers in a general sense is hard to say.[18] If actual political experiences did determine this choice of words, then these labels would have had quite an impact. Unquestionably, though, all of these Christians were outsiders in the world because of their distinct lifestyle and their allegiance to Jesus. Their spiritual life resulted in a different social life, one criticized by their neighbors. The letter repeatedly exhorts its readers to endure persecution and to live a life of holiness, humility, and integrity. As they maintained their good testimony, unbelievers would take notice and some would acknowledge God (2:12, 15; 3:1–2, 16).

Implications for Today

There are several lessons that 1 Peter offers Christians engaged in the immigration discussion. The first and most important is that migration is here taken as *a foundational metaphor* for what it means to be a Christian. In fact, this metaphor was prominent in the thinking of the early church.[19] What all Christians should appreciate is that the more they can grasp about migration and the experiences of immigrants, the more they will understand their faith—that is, the truths of such convictions as the reality of having another (heavenly) citizenship and the rejection that can come from being different, as well as the vulnerability that surfaces with needing to be dependent on God. Sadly, it is not uncommon for Christians to not feel like "strangers in a strange land"; their place of residence has lost its strangeness, and now they join others in wanting to keep strangers out.

The second lesson follows from the first. If majority-culture Christians do embrace the immigrant—whether documented or undocumented—this stance could mark them in a particular way as foreigners and strangers in that they would be going against the current of a good portion of public opinion. To take that stand on the basis of biblical convictions may lead to opposition from the broader majority culture. According to 1 Peter, to suffer for doing good is a privilege and part of the pilgrimage of faith.

All Christians, those of the majority culture and of Hispanic and other immigrant cultures, are foreigners and strangers in the world because of their faith. This is something they share. But there is another point here, and it echoes what has been mentioned earlier. Immigrant believers might identify with details of this biblical text through their analogous experiences.

Immigrants also are foreigners and strangers in this country in a physical, cultural, and social sense. Consequently, they can face rejection and discrimination in these spheres too, not just at the faith level. This second dimension of their experience as foreigners and strangers can add a richness to their reading of the epistle. If the hypotheses are correct that suggest the original recipients of the letter were actually social outcasts, then the Hispanic experience is close to what those early Christians went through; Hispanics may hear the apostle's words in a manner similar to its original audience. In these ways, Hispanic Christians might be able to contribute to the majority-culture Christians' understanding of the exhortations and promises of the Word of God.

The Call to Hospitality

New Testament Teaching

Chapter 3, the second part of our survey of the Old Testament, began with a discussion of hospitality in the ancient world and Israel. The practice of hospitality continued into the first century and beyond. In the New Testament, hospitality received an even greater impetus and was a prominent custom in the early church. Meals were shared and shelter provided to Christians and non-Christians, to friends, family, and strangers.[20]

In addition to the many examples of hospitality that can be found in the New Testament, the words of Jesus and exhortations in several letters are sources of teaching on the subject. The Gospel accounts describe a number of scenes where Jesus is in someone's home for a meal (a well-known example is the dinner party at Zacchaeus's house, Luke 19:1–10), but the teaching Jesus gives at a meal in a Pharisee's house in the Gospel of Luke, chapter 14, is the most relevant. When Jesus sees how guests at this dinner vie for places of prominence, he tells his host that the special guests at a banquet in God's sight would be the poor and the sick, those of no social standing who would not have the means to repay the gesture (Luke 14:12–14). Many verses urge Christians to offer a gracious welcome to others. These include Romans 12:13, Hebrews 13:2 (undoubtedly an allusion to Gen. 18 and 19), and 1 Peter 4:9. The virtue of hospitality was expected of the leadership of the Christian community (1 Tim. 3:2; Titus 1:8; cf. 1 Tim. 5:9–10).[21]

The early church gathered in homes to enjoy fellowship, meet their physical needs, and share meals. These small assemblies in an intimate context were a good setting for the practice of hospitality. The most profound opportunity to embody hospitality was and continues to be the celebration of the Lord's Supper. This meal is grounded in the sacrifice of Jesus on the cross and is rooted in his final meal with the disciples (Matt. 26:17–29 and parr.). If hospitality is about opening oneself up and giving oneself to others, if it is a time of sharing with all who claim the faith with the full expectation of God's provision, then the conjunction of the Lord's Supper and the cross is a powerful demonstration of divine hospitality. All are welcome. We who were once enemies of God have been reconciled to him and have been baptized into one body; all stand as equals before the Lord (Rom. 5:10; 1 Cor. 12:12–13; Gal. 3:27–29; Eph. 2). At the

Table, forgiven sinners embrace other sinners and forgive those who have committed transgressions against them (cf. Matt. 6:12; Luke 11:4). It is no wonder that Paul's instruction on the Lord's Supper in 1 Corinthians 11 combines concern for the outcasts and the unfortunate with the call to serious self-evaluation (vv. 17–34). The Lord's Supper, so central a symbol of the Christian faith and so important for nurturing the remembrance of the person and work of Jesus, was inseparable from the practice of hospitality.

Implications for Today

There is no need for me to add much more at this point to what has already been said in the previous chapter concerning hospitality and its relationship to the immigration discussion. The New Testament reinforces the importance and value of hospitality with what Jesus said and did and with the numerous directives in the epistles. Of course, for the Christian, the Lord's Supper is the consummate reminder of the need to be hospitable to others, even to those very different from ourselves, to the stranger in our midst. There at the Table any question of status or legality is superseded by the embrace of friends and family and fellow believers, by this visible expression and public declaration of the mercy, compassion, and provision of God.[22] To come periodically to the Table, yet without a commitment to kindness and openness to others, is to not do justice to its purpose and spirit. At the very least, the recognition of our sinfulness and of the boundless forgiveness of God should leaven Christian attitudes toward outsiders in need—even those whom we know are here as undocumented immigrants. This orientation in attitude does not solve the legal quandary, but it can impact the direction of the conversation and its tone in ways that resonate with this most important Christian practice.

What about Romans 13?

Why Romans 13 Now?

I have placed this New Testament text last by design.[23] In conversations I have had with students, friends, and others, Romans 13:1–7 is often brought up to argue against allowing entry to undocumented Hispanic immigrants. To cross the border without the proper permission is to break the law of the United States. Their presence in this country by definition, therefore, is illegal. In its crassest form, I have heard this as, "What is it about 'illegal' that you don't understand?" This wrong of violating the nation's borders should be penalized, it is said, and these lawbreakers should expect to suffer the consequences. Moreover, how can Hispanics who claim to be Christians so blatantly violate a clear teaching of Scripture?

If one begins here, any sensible discussion about Hispanic immigration is quickly aborted. Either one has proper documentation or not; either one tried to go through established channels, irrespective of what that actually entails, or not. Everything is trumped by legal status. It is my conviction, however, that there are a series of prior considerations that must be dealt with before introducing issues of legality. That is why this book looks at the breadth of biblical material on migration before engaging this passage. Of course one must treat legal matters, but at the most appropriate place in the discussion. The country does need to make some decisions and to organize itself on these issues. Responses to the challenges of immigration, though, should arise from a set of beliefs and commitments. For the Christian, these ultimately must be grounded in the full revelation found in the Bible.

If one begins with a biblical orientation that includes the centrality of the importance of the immigrant as made in the image of God, if one can appreciate how pervasive migration experiences are to the history and faith of the people of God, if Old Testament law projects an ethics of compassion, and if the thrust of Jesus's ministry and the New Testament as a whole is to love the outsider and be hospitable, then the inclination is to be charitable to the immigrant in the name of God and Christ. This inclination, in turn, will affect how one assesses present legislation and ponders where things should go from here at a personal level, within the local and national church and other Christian spheres, and finally throughout the country at every level of government. The tone of the conversation will be different, as will the kind of legislation that is brought forward.

If, on top of these fundamental faith convictions, one evaluates the history of immigration law in the United States as confused, contradictory, and in some ways unfair to the various affected parties, then that also will affect the perspective on the legality question. If one believes that these laws do not fit the teaching of the Bible and the ethical demands of the heart of God, some Christians will not say, "What is it about 'illegal' that you don't understand?"; instead, they might declare with the apostles Peter and John, "Which is right in God's eyes: to listen to you, or to him? You be the judges!" (Acts 4:19). In other words, can a Christian stance on immigration ignore the vast material in both Testaments concerning the outsider and be reduced simply to the issue of legal standing?

Before these statements raise all kinds of alarm, let me make it very clear that I am not advocating civil disobedience on a large scale, just as most Christians who have strong misgivings about undocumented immigrants are not lobbying for a massive national deportation operation to rid the country of one and all. It is a narrow understanding of the nature of law and the Christian's relationship to human government that I question.

Problems with Defaulting to Romans 13

Many Christians read Romans 13 with the unconscious assumption that the nation's laws are inherently good and just.

The sentiment is that to obey them is not only pleasing to God; it is common sense. We are a nation that believes in the "rule of law"! At one level, this statement is an obvious truism. Every nation in the history of the world has been run by a set of laws. We can go back thousands of years and find law codes. In fact, chapter 3 looked at one such law code, that of ancient Israel. Every country on the planet today has a system of laws. It is not enough, therefore, to simply declare that the United States follows a "rule of law." Rather, the deeper issue to consider is whether the legal system that is currently in place is good (in relationship to our Christian commitments) and practical and efficient (for the national benefit). In light of what has been covered in this book, current immigration law (unless immigration reform has been passed while this book was at press) is found wanting on all counts.

The need to begin with Romans 12. What can be missed is that Romans 12 prefaces Paul's words concerning human government. It contrasts the mind-set and life of Christians with what they encounter in society. Romans 12 exhorts believers not to be molded by the "pattern of this world" (12:1–2), which would include being shaped by the nation's political ideologies—in this case, with regard to immigration and the treatment of immigrants, as well as in relation to a host of other topics. Instead, Christians should have their minds renewed so as to know the will of God. The renewal of the mind about immigration based on Scripture has been a purpose of this book. Paul goes on to say that believers should humbly serve others, have compassion, and strive to live peaceably with everyone (12:3–18). He closes this section with a radical exhortation: we are to feed and give drink to our enemies (12:19–21; cf. Matt. 5:43–48; Luke 6:27–36). This is a strong word to those who are suspicious of certain immigrants. The lesson is this: even if immigrants are perceived to be "enemies," Christians are called to care for their needs. Indeed, US law does not prohibit charitable outreach to immigrants, even the undocumented. English learning classes, food and clothes pantries, after-school tutoring for children, recreational opportunities, legal orientation, and much more are permitted. Most people, though, are unaware of this fact.

Discerning submission, not blind obedience. With this backdrop we turn to Romans 13. The government is a different institution than the church; it has a different agenda and set of rules. How does the set of commitments in Romans 12 carry over to living in society under these conditions? Christians, Paul says, should respect the government. The text says "be subject" (or "submit," *hypotassō*) to the established authorities (13:1). Note that it does not say "obey." In other words, our appreciation of what any government pronounces or enacts has boundaries. This respect does not mean agreeing with or sanctifying everything a human government says and does. If one does not follow a law, there may be a sanction to which one must submit. The reason is that Christians must respond to a higher authority, to the Lord of the church (Matt. 28:18; Eph. 1:20–23; Phil. 2:9–11; Col. 1:15–18; Rev. 1:17–18; etc.), and to a higher law and set of values. There will be times when these two authorities will not agree. This is such a time. How to adjudicate these uncomfortable moments has occupied Christian theology for centuries.[24]

One of the wonderful privileges that the political system of the United States allows is the right to disagree with the government. Motivated by their principles, Christians do this all the time in multiple ways: at the ballot box; through publications; by organizing educational, legal, and civic organizations that would defend other points of view; by participating in peaceful protests of many kinds for a host of causes. I could go on. Each of these actions in its own way expresses reservations about the state of affairs and the things the government is mandating. Citizens are given opportunities to change legislation that is deemed inadequate or wrong. This is the history of politics in this country. One powerful example was the overturning of segregation laws through the efforts of the civil rights movement. These changes are difficult; they generate debates and reveal conflicting agendas. That is the nature of life in democracy.

The US government itself recognizes that it must change its immigration legislation. The national leadership from across the political spectrum and the country as a whole know that what is in place now is not working and must be revised or replaced.

The US government itself recognizes that it must change its legislation.

The various recent attempts to craft a new comprehensive immigration policy are evidence of the need for different laws to deal with current immigration challenges.

In sum, to quote Romans 13 on the immigration issue without nuance or biblical and historical depth simply will not do. I am arguing that Christians should search the Scriptures for guidance in evaluating the development of immigration policy and engaging its multifaceted set of problems. From that foundation, Christians could begin to move forward to the legal issues. Discussion on legality cannot be limited just to questions about complying with the present laws. If the laws are problematic theologically, humanely, and pragmatically—and since everyone agrees that reform must come—the call to submit to the authorities in Romans 13 can be processed in fresh and constructive ways. Respect for the nation's present laws is coupled with and informed by the move toward a new set of laws. As Christians participate in this change, in whatever fashion, they should do so self-consciously *as Christians*.

Immigrants and Romans 13

I would like to offer some observations concerning how Hispanic believers who are undocumented immigrants respond to

Romans 13. Of course, there would be those who set aside the passage on exegetical, theological, and pastoral grounds. My experience, however, is with Hispanic Christians primarily of the evangelical and Pentecostal streams. They would take this biblical text seriously, but their view is complex.

These Christians recognize that they are in violation of current law by living and working here. At the same time, they have experienced personally the law's contradictions and inequities. For example, the government turns a blind eye to many employers because the country needs the cheap labor, but then closes the door to social services on these same workers. Immigrants also respect the legal system of the United States for its efficiency and fairness in many areas. Many pay taxes, and they do their best to obey the laws of the land in every area that does not threaten their jobs, homes, and children's education. I have heard many express a desire to be model "citizens" as part of their Christian duty and in order to gain the respect of the majority culture. Finally, all wish for a legal resolution of the situation. Their hope is that the law itself will be reformed in such a way that their legal status is no longer an issue.

A Closing Thought

In the well-known Great Commission mandate of Matthew 28:18–20 (cf. Mark 16:15; Luke 24:44–49; Acts 1:8) the disciples are told to go to all the nations and make disciples. The book of Acts presents the account of how early believers crossed all sorts of borders and ventured into a variety of cultural contexts to preach the good news and establish churches. In some cases, these congregations and ministry teams were multicultural (e.g., Acts 13:1). This movement to a broader vision of the people of God was hard for many of the original Jewish Christians. The need to call a council to discuss the matter is proof of that

(Acts 15), as is Paul's need to rebuke the apostle Peter (whose cross-cultural actions are recorded in Acts 10–11) for distancing himself from gentile believers (Gal. 2:11–14).

Revelation describes a wonderful scene of the multilingual, multicultural, and multinational people of God singing praises in heaven to the Father and to the Lamb (Rev. 7:9–17). That is the goal to which the church should strive. Until then we must learn to live out the truth that there is neither Jew nor Greek; all are one in Christ (Gal. 3:28), because the walls of separation have come down (Eph. 2:11–22).

What has happened in the last few decades is that the world has come to these shores. The theological and pastoral—and yes, personal—challenge is to embrace this new reality of the presence of immigrants from around the globe as an opportunity to embody these biblical ideals in fresh ways. Many who have come are fellow Christians, and others will be exposed to the faith after they arrive. The way of seeing beyond the present tensions and problems of immigration to the heavenly vision and Paul's ideal is not easy; it was not easy for the early church. But it is good and right.

—⚬— 5 —⚬—

Where Do We Go from Here?

Final Thoughts

Hispanic immigration to the United States is a complex phenomenon. It has a history that extends back over 160 years. This history is not only about the movement of people across borders; it is also the story of complicated legislation and diverse cultural reactions. The number of immigrants, documented and undocumented, who have entered the country during the past thirty years has made this phenomenon the focus of national debate at many levels and in all sorts of arenas. This debate has been heated, and it has generated interesting alliances that cross traditional ideological lines. Those who have favored more restrictive immigration policies are nativists, environmentalists, low-skilled laborers who feel threatened, some unions, and citizens fearful about national security, the economic viability of social services, and the future of the reigning cultural identity. Those who have favored a more open strategy include free-market thinkers, business and agricultural interests, the

AFL-CIO, human rights organizations and activists, and much of academia. Strange bedfellows indeed!

Christians, of course, are members of this society and locate themselves at different points along this broad spectrum of opinion. When I have engaged Christians in conversation about immigration, I have found that more often than not this choice has had little to do with Christian convictions and much to do with ideological commitments and personal background and experience. This book attempts to offer what appears to be lacking: a biblical and theological framework from which Christians, *as Christians*, might participate in the ongoing debate.

At Two Borders

As I explained in the introduction, the title *Christians at the Border* carries two meanings. On the one hand, Christians in the United States all stand at the border with Mexico in a sociopolitical and economic sense. Everyone needs to make a decision about a host of concrete realities related to Hispanic immigration. That decision will influence how one treats Hispanics in the encounters of everyday life and how one expresses that point of view in the political arena. To meet the need to be informed about these kinds of issues, chapter 1 outlined a history of Hispanic immigration and summarized the principal arguments revolving around two of the more salient issues: cultural identity and the economic impact of immigration. These topics are broader and more intricate than many suppose, so the chapter presented additional perspectives on these two issues and then closed by including a third that often is ignored: Hispanic Christianity. Among Hispanic immigrants are millions of believers, so a Christian consideration of the national debate must take account of their presence.

The imposing array of problems and challenges should drive Christians to seek the wisdom of God. Chapters 2 through 4, then, surveyed the relevant biblical material. These chapters do not pretend to be exhaustive nor is the discussion (hopefully!) overly technical. My goal has been to demonstrate to the reader the wealth of divine revelation relevant to the topic of immigration. Chapter 2 began with a discussion of the image of God and subsequently cited a multitude of passages that portray migrants in the Old Testament. Chapter 3 continued in the Old Testament, moving from a consideration of the theme of hospitality to a treatment of Old Testament law. Chapter 4 turned to the New Testament. It began with the experiences and teaching of Jesus and then briefly dealt with the phrase "foreigners and strangers" in 1 Peter, revisited the theme of hospitality, and responded to objections that may arise from a particular interpretation of Romans 13.

Throughout these chapters, the biblical presentations were followed by a section titled "Implications for Today." The purpose of these reflections was to attempt to put the Bible and the situation of Hispanic immigration in dialogue. The survey of biblical material and these reflections place Christians at another, metaphorical, border. We must *all* make a decision about how to respond to the Bible's teaching and the example of Jesus. There is a threshold to cross, a road of obedience to travel.

If crossing that border transforms how majority-culture Christians view immigrants and immigration, and if it shapes how immigrants understand their life, privileges, and responsibilities in this country, then this crossing leads all back to that first border. The political boundary with Mexico now takes on a greater significance at the boundary of faith.

The Purpose of This Book

There is much this book does not cover. The sphere of the social, political, and economic is huge. The opening chapter is simply a doorway into these vast realms of data, opinions, and policy. The scope of the biblical discussion can also be daunting. The endnotes for each chapter and the appendix are designed to refer the interested reader to other resources.

This book also does not propose any legislative solutions, economic panaceas, or advice on cultural negotiations. *Christians at the Border* above all else strives to motivate believers of the majority culture and Hispanics to begin thinking, talking, and acting *as Christians* in regard to immigration. What I have written here is a starter, a primer that can serve as an orientation for grounding their views in the Bible. I do not aspire to anything more. If, through the grace of God, it can stimulate further biblical and theological reflection, as well as impact the tone and direction of the debate and legislation, then it will have served its purpose.

Final Thoughts

Resident Aliens is the provocative title of a stimulating work on Christian identity and ministry in modern America by Stanley Hauerwas and William Willimon.[1] The idea for the title apparently came from one of the biblical quotations that preface the book: "But our citizenship is in heaven" (Phil. 3:20–21). The title is apropos to our concerns, as "resident aliens" is one of the translations given for the Hebrew and Greek words that refer to sojourners in the Bible. *Resident Aliens*, however, does not deal at all with immigration issues (it was published in 1989). Nevertheless, what it says is relevant.

Hauerwas and Willimon's contention is that the Christian church has lost its way and is captive to the culture. The church must regain the vision of being a distinct community, a distinct community made up of ordinary individuals (resident aliens) with a calling to be faithful to its Lord. The focus on living the life of the Savior in the world is clear from the other biblical quotation that begins their book: "Have the same mindset as Christ Jesus" (Phil. 2:5). Christians are to display the life of Jesus, and this requires acquiring a set of virtues, like peaceableness, kindness, hospitality, and patience. Christians and the church need to be a certain kind of people with a particular way of looking at and living within society. For the church to be the church requires training in these virtues, the nurturing of Christian tradition through Word and sacrament, and the continual practice of the virtues.

The virtues are fundamental for a Christian approach to Hispanic immigration within the church and in the public square.[2] An appropriate response to the complicated situation in society will not come from detached, objective analysis, cost-benefit calculations, efficiency quotients, and cultural arguments. The decisions that are made and courses of action that are recommended should be commensurate with the life of Jesus—his actions, his teaching, his cross. Analysis and calculations are necessary, but they must be informed by more transcendent beliefs and other overriding life commitments.

This trajectory also requires reading the Scripture virtuously—that is, learning to read the Bible in such a way as to become the kind of person that is exemplified in the best characters of the text.[3] This person would read the Scriptures with humility, wisdom, and charity. Such readers, such Christian readers, can engage those of differing views on controversial topics (like immigration) in an edifying and constructive way, even as they grow in these same virtues toward the moral vision of the Bible.

Christians, both of the majority culture and Hispanic, are not to exclude the "other," whether Christian or non-Christian.[4] We are all called to embrace the "other." We can embrace those who are different—and even those who have offended or wronged us—because we have embraced Jesus, who calls us to a self-sacrificing life for others. We embrace him, because he first embraced us. We take up that cross of forgiveness and hospitality because he took up his.

This embrace of the other—the majority culture by the Hispanic and the Hispanic by the majority culture—will be a "soft embrace." The resident aliens of the majority culture (1 Pet. 2:11) will embrace the resident aliens from elsewhere. Both will be respectful and mindful of cultural differences, open to grow and change. This transformation will be reciprocal and mutual,

An appropriate response to the complicated situation in society will not come from detached, objective analysis, cost-benefit calculations, efficiency quotients, and cultural arguments.

personal and communal, in confidence of moving toward the common good, yet with great risk. Assured of the teaching of the Word, the empowerment of the Spirit, the example of Jesus, and the blessing of the Father, Christians can be the light of the Triune God in this national confusion that sometimes can be so dark. Let the journey to reconciliation begin. May the church lead the way.

The journey does not end when new legislation is passed. If it has not been finalized by this book's publication, it will happen soon enough. But these laws will be the fruit of negotiation and compromise; they will be both imperfect, because of competing agendas, and inescapably inadequate, however well intentioned. The deeper matters of the heart, of suspicion and worry by all sides, will continue after the passage of immigration reform. The mandate of the church to be a haven for the stranger and a household of the faithful of all cultures, though, will still need to be fleshed out daily in our homes, congregations, and communities, as well as at national levels. May we willingly take up the mantle of hospitality in light of the cross and move forward steadfastly in obedience with all grace and wisdom.

Afterword

Ronald J. Sider

*President Emeritus,
Evangelicals for Social Action*

Danny Carroll's book is even more important in 2013 than when it was first published in 2008. In those intervening years, major national efforts at comprehensive immigration reform failed and millions suffered. Despair over the possibility of comprehensive reform was widespread by 2012.

Today, however, things are suddenly much more hopeful. It is now widely thought that comprehensive immigration reform is politically possible—but only if large numbers of citizens lobby Congress to demand action. Carroll's book is an excellent tool for encouraging that action.

This new edition brings the reader up to date on the historical and legal information and expands the biblical material.

In the years since 2008, Danny Carroll and I have worked together in an important dialogue in Catholics and Evangelicals for the Common Good. Carroll contributed important scholarly material for that conversation. The agreement among Catholics and evangelicals that emerged in those conversations on immigration reform mirrors a developing consensus among a large number of widely diverse Christian leaders that comprehensive immigration reform is a biblically grounded imperative. This book helps readers understand why.

But it is still true that the plight of undocumented immigrants is one of the thorniest issues on our national landscape today. It continues to provoke very heated debates. How refreshing it is, then, to have Danny Carroll, an author who is sympathetic to both the immigrant and the host culture, call Christians to find a fresh starting point for the debate.

Carroll rightly reminds us of the complexities of the historical, cultural, and economic dimensions of immigration. These dimensions give rise to much of the rhetoric that we hear today (from both sides). But Carroll is absolutely right to insist that for Christians there is another even more important dimension that must be considered—that of our Christian faith. Many of the millions who have crossed America's southern border in recent years, with or without proper documentation, are Christians. Surely the faith of the immigrants, and the faith of Christians in the host culture, must be decisive in the way churches, communities, and individual believers think about and respond to the political and social realities of the current immigration crisis.

The Bible is the most important place to look for guidance. I agree with Carroll that Christians—both immigrants and those in the majority culture—must look at the issue through biblical lenses. Those lenses remind us first of all that these debates are about people—people made in the image of God, with all the inherent worth and standing that lofty designation entails. Policy debates, statistics, spreadsheets, and economic outcomes can often cloud this simple fact that we must ever keep before us.

As we look in the Old Testament we are reminded of the people of God who many times crossed national boundaries. We also see plentiful evidence of God's persistent and profound love for the needy and the disenfranchised. The biblical record also shows how the people of God lived out their faith while sojourning and how God legislated the behavior of outsiders who came to live with his people. The Old Testament record, then, speaks to both populations, calling for hospitality, grace, and faith as we think and work together toward political and economic solutions.

As we move to the New Testament and the life of Jesus, we see Jesus's ongoing example of proactive consideration for the marginalized in society, the outsiders. Later in the New Testament, 1 Peter confronts us with the fact that all Christians are "foreigners and strangers" in this world because of their faith. We must, therefore, look at societal issues differently. We're not driven primarily by political or economic expediencies or by partisan rhetoric but by a new set of values, a kingdom way of living on planet earth. Our citizenship in Christ's kingdom transcends the differences in our earthly nationalities. As Christians think about Hispanic immigration, our approach must be grounded in that citizenship. And the courses of action we recommend must be in line with biblical teaching.

The final chapter title asks where we go from here. Let's follow Danny Carroll in going to the Bible. Let's join him in thinking biblically and theologically about this issue of great national import. Let's find distinctively Christian approaches to meeting such obvious human needs. Let's energize our churches and our communities, finding ways to work toward practices and policies that honor the dignity of every human and that demonstrate the love of God to all who observe our words and actions.

Appendix

Selected Resources

The amount of literature on immigration is exploding, and the internet sites dedicated to issues concerning immigration continue to multiply. What follows is limited to *a selection* of this burgeoning number of resources. Since this listing cannot be exhaustive, I have tried to make it representative of different viewpoints. I also have limited the following to resources in English. Additional resources appear in the notes.

Sociological, Economic, and Political Studies

Bacon, David. *Illegal People: How Globalization Creates Migration and Criminalizes Immigrants*. Boston: Beacon, 2008.

Borjas, George J., ed. *Mexican Immigration to the United States*. National Bureau of Economic Research Conference Report. Chicago: University of Chicago Press, 2007.

Brettell, Caroline B., and James F. Hollifield, eds. *Migration Theory: Talking across Disciplines*. 2nd ed. New York: Routledge, 2008.

Buchanan, Patrick J. *State of Emergency: The Third World Invasion and Conquest of America*. New York: Thomas Dunne, 2006.

Bush, Jeb, and Clint Bolick. *Immigration Wars: Forging an American Solution*. New York: Threshold Editions, 2013.

Castles, Stephen, and Mark J. Miller. *The Age of Migration: International Population Movements in the Modern World*. 4th ed. New York: Guilford, 2009.

Fitzgerald, David. *A Nation of Emigrants: How Mexico Manages Its Migration*. Berkeley: University of California Press, 2009.

Fox, Vicente, with Rob Allyn. *Revolution of Hope: The Life, Faith, and Dreams of a Mexican President*. New York: Viking, 2007.

Haerens, Margaret, ed. *Illegal Immigration: Opposing Viewpoints*. Opposing Viewpoints Series. Detroit: Thomson Gale, 2006.

Hanson, Gordon H. *Why Does Immigration Divide America? Public Finance and Political Opposition to Open Borders*. Washington, DC: Institute for International Economics, 2005.

Higham, John. *Strangers in the Land: Patterns of American Nativism, 1860–1925*. 2nd ed. New Brunswick, NJ: Rutgers University Press, 2002.

Huntington, Samuel P. *Who Are We? The Challenges to America's National Identity*. New York: Simon & Schuster, 2004.

Krikorian, Mark. *The New Case against Immigration: Both Legal and Illegal*. New York: Sentinel, 2008.

Laufer, Peter. *Wetback Nation: The Case for Opening the Mexican-American Border*. Chicago: Ivan R. Dee, 2004.

Levitt, Peggy. *God Needs No Passport: Immigrants and the Changing American Religious Landscape*. New York: New Press, 2007.

MacDonald, Heather, Victor Davis Hanson, and Steven Malanga. *The Immigration Solution: A Better Plan than Today's*. Chicago: Ivan R. Dee, 2007.

Massey, Douglas S., ed. *New Faces in New Places: The Changing Geography of American Immigration*. New York: Russell Sage Foundation, 2008.

Massey, Douglas S., Jorge Durand, and Nolan J. Malone. *Beyond Smoke and Mirrors: Mexican Immigration in an Era of Economic Integration*. New York: Russell Sage Foundation, 2002.

Portes, Alejandro, and Rubén G. Rumbaut. *Immigrant America: A Portrait*. 3rd ed. Berkeley: University of California Press, 2006.

Pritchett, Lant. *Let Their People Come: Breaking the Gridlock on Global Labor Mobility*. Washington, DC: Center for Global Development, 2006.

Rivera, Geraldo. *HISpanic: Why Americans Fear Hispanics in the U.S.* New York: Celebra, 2008.

Smith, Robert Courtney. *Mexican New York: Transnational Lives of New Immigrants*. Berkeley: University of California Press, 2006.

Tancredo, Tom. *In Mortal Danger: The Battle for America's Border and Security*. Nashville: WND Books, 2006.

Zolberg, Aristide R. *A Nation by Design: Immigration Policy in the Fashioning of America*. New York: Russell Sage Foundation; Cambridge, MA: Harvard University Press, 2007.

Hispanic Experience: Crossing the Border and Life in the United States (Autobiography, Reporting, and Realistic Cultural Fiction)

Álvarez, Julia. *How the García Girls Lost Their Accent*. New York: Plume, 1992.

———. *Once upon a Quinceañera: Coming of Age in the U.S.A.* New York: Viking, 2007.

Cisneros, Sandra. *Caramelo or Puro Cuento*. New York: Vintage, 2002.

Ferguson, Kathryn, Norma A. Price, and Ted Parks. *Crossing with the Virgin: Stories from the Migrant Trail*. Tucson: University of Arizona Press, 2010.

Gaynor, Tim. *Midnight on the Line: The Secret Life of the U.S.-Mexican Border*. New York: St. Martin's Press, 2009.

Hagan, Jacqueline María. *Migration Miracle: Faith, Hope, and Meaning on the Undocumented Journey*. Cambridge, MA: Harvard University Press, 2008.

Martínez, Rubén. *Crossing Over: A Mexican Family on the Migrant Trail*. New York: Metropolitan Books, 2001.

Nazario, Sonia. *Enrique's Journey*. New York: Random House, 2006.

Ramos, Jorge. *Dying to Cross: The Worst Immigrant Tragedy in American History*. Translated by K. Cordero. New York: Rayo, 2005.

———. *The Other Face of America: Chronicles of the Immigrants Shaping Our Future*. Translated by P. J. Duncan. New York: Rayo, 2002.

Rodríguez, Richard. *Brown: The Last Discovery of America*. New York: Penguin, 2002.

Rose, Ananda. *Showdown in the Desert: Religion, Law, and the Immigration Controversy*. New York: Oxford University Press, 2012.

Thompson, Gabriel. *Working in the Shadows: A Year of Doing the Jobs (Most) Americans Won't Do*. New York: Nation Books, 2010.

Thorpe, Helen. *Just Like Us: The True Story of Four Mexican Girls Coming of Age in America*. New York: Scribner, 2009.

Urrea, Luis Alberto. *The Devil's Highway: A True Story*. New York: Back Bay Books, 2004.

———. *Into the Beautiful North: A Novel*. New York: Back Bay Books, 2009.

Villaseñor, Victor. *Burro Genius: A Memoir*. New York: HarperCollins, 2004.

Biblical and Theological Resources

Biblical and Theological Studies

Achenbach, Reinhard, Rainer Albertz, and Jakob Wöhrle, eds. *The Foreigner and the Law: Perspectives from the Hebrew Bible and the Ancient Near*

East. Beihefte zur Zeitschrift für Altorientalische und Biblische Rechtsge-schichte 16. Wiesbaden: Harrassowitz, 2011.

Azaransky, Sarah, ed. *Religion and Politics in America's Borderlands*. Lanham, MD: Lexington Books, 2013.

Bietenhard, H., and F. S. Rothenberg. "Foreign, Alien, Dispersion, Stranger." In *The New International Dictionary of New Testament Theology*, edited by Colin Brown, vol. 1, 683–92. Grand Rapids: Zondervan, 1975.

Block, Daniel I. "Sojourner." In *International Standard Bible Encyclopaedia*, edited by G. W. Bromiley, vol. 4, 561–64. Rev. ed. Grand Rapids: Eerdmans, 1988.

Carroll R., M. Daniel. "Aliens, Immigration, and Refugees." In *Dictionary of Scripture and Ethics*, edited by J. B. Green, 53–58. Grand Rapids: Baker Academic, 2011.

———. "Biblical Perspectives on Migration and Mission: Contributions from the Old Testament." *Mission Studies* 30, no. 1 (2013): 9–24.

———. "How to Shape Christian Perspectives on Immigration? Strategies for Communicating Biblical Teaching." In *Religion and Politics in America's Borderlands*, edited by S. Azaransky, 57–77. Lanham, MD: Lexington Books, 2013.

———. "Immigration: Looking at the Challenges through a Missional Lens." In *Living Witness: Explorations in Missional Ethics*, edited by J. Rowe and A. Draycott, 258–77. Downers Grove, IL: InterVarsity, 2012.

———. "Reading the Bible through Other Lenses: New Vistas from a Hispanic Diaspora Perspective." In *Global Voices: Reading the Bible in the Majority World*, edited by C. S. Keener and M. D. Carroll R., 5–26. Peabody, MA: Hendrickson, 2012.

———. "Welcoming the Stranger: Toward a Theology of Immigration in Deu-teronomy." In *For Our Good Always: Studies on the Message and Influence of Deuteronomy in Honor of Daniel I. Block*, edited by J. S. DeRouchie, J. Gile, and K. J. Turner, 441–61. Winona Lake, IN: Eisenbrauns, 2013.

Daniel, Ben. *Neighbor: Christian Encounters with "Illegal" Immigration*. Louisville: Westminster John Knox, 2010.

Ekblad, Bob. *Reading the Bible with the Damned*. Louisville: Westminster John Knox, 2005.

Gowan, Donald E. "Wealth and Poverty in the Old Testament: The Case of the Widow, the Orphan, and the Sojourner." *Interpretation* 41, no. 4 (1987): 341–53.

Groody, Daniel G., and Gioacchino Campese, eds. *A Promised Land, A Perilous Journey: Theological Perspectives on Migration*. Notre Dame: University of Notre Dame Press, 2008.

Heyer, Kristin E. *Kinship across Borders: A Christian Ethic of Immigration*. Washington, DC: Georgetown University Press, 2012.

Hoffmeier, James K. *The Immigration Crisis: Immigrants, Aliens, and the Bible*. Wheaton: Crossway, 2009.

Kellermann, D. "*gûr*." In *Theological Dictionary of the Old Testament*, edited by G. J. Botterweck and H. Ringgren, vol. 2, 439–49. Grand Rapids: Eerdmans, 1975.

Knauth, R. J. D. "Alien, Foreign Resident." In *Dictionary of the Old Testament: Pentateuch*, edited by T. Desmond Alexander and David W. Baker, 26–33. Downers Grove, IL: InterVarsity, 2003.

Lee Cuellar, Gregory. *Voices of Marginality: Exile and Return in Second Isaiah 40–55 and the Mexican Immigrant Experience*. American University Studies, Series VII, vol. 271. New York: Peter Lang, 2008.

Miller, Patrick D. "Israel as Host to Strangers." In *Israelite Religion and Biblical Theology: Collected Essays*, edited by Patrick D. Miller, 548–71. Journal for the Study of the Old Testament Supplement Series 267. Sheffield: Sheffield Academic Press, 2000.

Myers, Ched, and Matthew Colwell. *Our God Is Undocumented: Biblical Faith and Immigrant Justice*. St. Louis: Chalice, 2012.

O'Neil, William R., and William C. Spohn. "Rights of Passage: The Ethics of Immigration and Refugee Policy." *Theological Studies* 59, no. 1 (1998): 84–106.

Pohl, Christine D. "Responding to Strangers: Insights from the Christian Tradition." *Studies in Christian Ethics* 19, no. 1 (2006): 81–101.

Ramírez Kidd, José E. *Alterity and Identity in Israel: The Ger in the Old Testament*. Beihefte zur Zeitschrift für die alttestamentliche Wissenschaft 283. Berlin: de Gruyter, 1999.

Ruiz, Jean-Pierre. *Reading from the Edges: The Bible & People on the Move*. Maryknoll, NY: Orbis, 2011.

Schmidt, K. L., M. A. Schmidt, and R. Meyer. "*paroikos*." In *Theological Dictionary of the New Testament*, edited by Gerhard Friedrich, vol. 5, 841–53. Translated by Geoffrey W. Bromiley. Grand Rapids: Eerdmans, 1967.

Snyder, Susanna. *Asylum-Seeking, Migration and Church*. Explorations in Practical, Pastoral and Empirical Theology. Burlington, VT: Ashgate, 2012.

Spina, F. A. "Israelites as *gerim*: Sojourners in Social and Historical Context." In *The Word of the Lord Shall Go Forth: Essays in Honor of David Noel Freedman in Celebration of His Sixtieth Birthday*, edited by C. L. Meyers and M. O'Connor, 321–35. Winona Lake, IN: Eisenbrauns, 1983.

Wan, Enoch. *Diaspora Missiology: Theory, Methodology, and Practice*. Portland, OR: Institute of Diaspora Studies, 2011.

Wilbanks, Dana W. *Re-creating America: The Ethics of U.S. Immigration and Refugee Policy in a Christian Perspective*. Nashville: Abingdon, 1996.

Hispanic (Latino/a) Theology and Ministry

PUBLICATIONS

Aponte, Edwin. *¡Santo! Varieties of Latino/a Spirituality*. Maryknoll, NY: Orbis, 2012.

Aponte, Edwin, and Miguel A. de la Torre, eds. *Handbook of Latino/a Theologies*. St. Louis: Chalice, 2006.

Badillo, David A. *Latinos and the New Immigrant Church*. Baltimore: Johns Hopkins University Press, 2006.

Crespo, Orlando. *Being Latino in Christ: Finding Wholeness in Your Ethnic Identity*. Downers Grove, IL: InterVarsity, 2003.

Elizondo, Virgilio P. *Galilean Journey: The Mexican-American Promise*. Rev. ed. Maryknoll, NY: Orbis, 2000.

Espín, Orlando O. *The Faith of the People: Theological Reflections on Popular Catholicism*. Maryknoll, NY: Orbis, 1997.

González, Justo L. *Mañana: Christian Theology from a Hispanic Perspective*. Nashville: Abingdon, 1990.

———. *Santa Biblia: The Bible through Hispanic Eyes*. Nashville: Abingdon, 1996.

Isasi-Díaz, Ada María. *La Lucha Continues: Mujerista Theology*. Maryknoll, NY: Orbis, 2004.

Maldonado, David, Jr., ed. *Protestantes/Protestants: Hispanic Christianity within Mainline Traditions*. Nashville: Abingdon, 1999.

Martínez, Juan Francisco. *Los Protestantes: An Introduction to Latino Protestantism in the United States*. Santa Barbara, CA: Praeger, 2011.

———. *Walk with the People: Latino Ministry in the United States*. Nashville: Abingdon, 2008.

Nanko-Fernández, Carmen. *Theologizing in Spanglish*. Maryknoll, NY: Orbis, 2010.

Padilla, Alvin, Roberto Goizueta, and Eldin Villafañe, eds. *Hispanic Christian Thought at the Dawn of the Twenty-First Century: Apuntes in Honor of Justo L. González*. Nashville: Abingdon, 2005.

Pedraja, Luis G. *Teología: An Introduction to Hispanic Theology*. Nashville: Abingdon, 2003.

Recinos, Harold J. *Good News from the Barrio: Prophetic Witness for the Church*. Louisville: Westminster John Knox, 2006.

Rivera-Rodríguez, Luis. "Toward a Diaspora Hermeneutics (Hispanic North America)." In *Character Ethics and the Old Testament: Moral Dimensions of Scripture*, edited by M. Daniel Carroll R. and Jacqueline Lapsley, 169–89. Louisville: Westminster John Knox, 2007.

JOURNALS

Apuntes

Journal of Hispanic/Latino Theology

Journal of Latin American Theology: Christian Reflections from the Latino South

Internet Sites

US Government

US Census Bureau: www.census.gov/newsroom

US Citizenship and Immigration Services: www.uscis.gov/portal/site/uscis; www.us-immigration.com

US Department of Homeland Security: www.dhs.gov

Sympathetic to Hispanic Immigration

ACTIVIST ORGANIZATIONS

America's Voice: http://americasvoiceonline.org

BorderLinks: www.borderlinks.org

Coalition for Comprehensive Immigration Reform: www.cirnow.org

Immigrant Solidarity Network: www.immigrantsolidarity.org

League of United Latin American Citizens: www.lulac.org

Mexican American Legal Defense and Education Fund: www.maldef.org

National Council of La Raza: www.nclr.org

National Immigration Forum: www.immigrationforum.org

National Network for Immigration and Refugee Rights: www.nnirr.org

No More Deaths: www.nomoredeaths.org

THINK TANKS AND RESEARCH CENTERS[1]

Immigration Legal Resource Center: www.ilrc.org

Mexican Migration Project: http://mmp.opr.princeton.edu

Migration Policy Institute: www.migrationpolicy.org

Pew Hispanic Center: www.pewhispanic.org

Urban Institute: www.urban.org/immigrants

Opposed to Hispanic Immigration

ACTIVIST ORGANIZATIONS

Americans for Immigration Control: www.immigrationcontrol.com

Americans for Legal Immigration: www.alipac.us

Immigration's Human Cost: www.immigrationshumancost.org

Minuteman Civil Defense Corps: www.minutemanhq.com

The Minuteman Project: www.minutemanproject.com

US Border Control: www.usbc.org

Think Tanks and Research Centers

Center for Immigration Studies: www.cis.org

Federation for American Immigration Reform: www.fairus.org

Heritage Foundation: www.heritage.org/issues/immigration

Sierrans for US Population Stabilization: www.susps.org

Religious Organizations and Coalitions

American Baptist Churches: http://abhms.org/justice_ministries/immigration_and_refugee_services/

American Friends Service Committee: https://afsc.org/project/immigrants-rights

Christian Coalition of America: www.cc.org

Christians for Comprehensive Immigration Reform: www.faithandimmigration.org

Church World Service: http://hunger.cwsglobal.org/site/PageServer?pagename=action_what_assist_main

Conservatives for Comprehensive Immigration Reform: www.cfcir.org

Esperanza USA: www.esperanzaamerica.com

Evangelical Covenant Church: www.covchurch.org/resolutions/2013-immigration

Evangelical Free Church: http://immigranthope.org

Evangelical Immigration Table: http://evangelicalimmigrationtable.com

Evangelical Lutheran Church in America: www.elca.org/What-We-Believe/Social-Issues/Resolutions/Comprehensive-Immigration-Reform.aspx

Hispanic Coalition for Comprehensive Immigration Reform: www.hispaniccoalitionforcir.com

G92: http://g92.org

Lutheran Church—Missouri Synod: www.lcms.org/ctcr

Lutheran Immigration and Refugee Service: http://lirs.org

Mennonite Church USA: www.mennoniteusa.org/executive-board/immigration

National Association of Evangelicals: www.nae.net/government-relations/for-the-health-of-the-nation/human-rights/immigration-reform

National Council of Christian Churches: www.churchworldservice.org/Immigration

National Hispanic Christian Leadership Conference: www.nhclc.org

Presbyterian Church (USA): http://oga.pcusa.org/section/departments/immigration/

Reformed Church of America: www.rca.org/sslpage.aspx?pid=504

Sojourners Community: http://sojo.net/topics/racial-and-social-justice/immigration

Southern Baptist Convention: www.sbc.net/resolutions/amResolution.asp?ID=1213

Southern Baptist Convention Ethics and Religious Liberty Commission: http://erlc.com/topics/C55

United Methodist Church: www.umc.org/site/c.lwL4KnN1LtH/b.7679333/k.6E87/The_Church_and_Immigration.htm

United States Catholic Church:

Catholic Campaign for Immigration Reform: www.justiceforimmigrants.org/index.shtml

Catholic Legal Immigration Network, Inc.: http://cliniclegal.org

Conference of Catholic Bishops: www.usccb.org/about/migration-and-refugee-services/

"Strangers No Longer: Together on the Journey of Hope": www.usccb.org/issues-and-action/human-life-and-dignity/immigration/strangers-no-longer-together-on-the-journey-of-hope.cfm

Professional Hispanic Christian Scholarly Associations

Academy of Catholic Hispanic Theologians of the United States (ACHTUS): www.achtus.org

Asociación para la Educación Teológica Hispana (AETH): www.aeth.org

Hispanic Theological Initiative (HTI): www.ptsem.edu/hti/

Notes

Introduction

1. For the impact of the war, see Proyecto Interdiocesano Recuperación de la Memoria Histórica/Catholic Institute for International Relations, *Guatemala: Never Again* (Maryknoll, NY: Orbis, 1999).

2. See, from 2010, www.pewforum.org/Politics-and-Elections/Few-Say-Religion -Shapes-Immigration-Environment-Views.aspx.

3. The Department of Education began using the term "Hispanic" in 1965 to refer to a category of students who could receive aid under Title IV of the Higher Education Act of 1965. There is conflicting testimony on the web as to when the Census Bureau introduced the term—either 1970 or 1980. For government documents, including definitions of the category "Hispanic," see www .census.gov/population/www/socdemo/compraceho.html; www.whitehouse.gov /omb/fedreg/1997standards.html; http://quickfacts.census.gov/qfd/meta/long _RHI825211.htm. A collection of reports that demonstrates the interplay of differences and commonalities is Jorge Ramos, *The Other Face of America: Chronicles of the Immigrants Shaping Our Future*, trans. P. J. Duncan (New York: Rayo, 2002).

The choice of an appropriate label also is discussed among Hispanic theologians. See, for example, Fernando F. Segovia, "Aliens in the Promised Land: The Manifest Destiny of U.S. Hispanic American Theology," in *Hispanic/Latino Theology: Challenge and Promise*, ed. Ada María Isasi-Díaz and Fernando F. Segovia (Minneapolis: Fortress, 1996), 15–42 (see esp. 31–42).

4. Another term is *Chicano* (feminine *Chicana*). This word is limited to those of Mexican descent and can be associated with a more militant approach to Mexican-American ethnicity.

5. Still another category is the "internally displaced." This category includes those who flee from an area of conflict but remain within the boundaries of their country.

Chapter 1: Hispanic Immigration

1. Jorge Ramos, *Dying to Cross: The Worst Immigrant Tragedy in American History*, trans. K. Cordero (New York: Rayo, 2005). The driver, Tyrone Williams,

was convicted in January 2007 of fifty-eight counts of conspiracy and of harboring and transporting immigrants. He was sentenced to life without parole. Ironically, Williams is an immigrant from Jamaica.

2. "The Death of Lance Corporal Gutiérrez," CBS News, April 23, 2003, www .cbsnews.com/2100-500164_162-550779.html.

3. For example, Rubén Martínez, *Crossing Over: A Mexican Family on the Migrant Trail* (New York: Metropolitan Books, 2001); Luis Alberto Urrea, *The Devil's Highway: A True Story* (New York: Back Bay Books, 2004); Sonia Nazario, *Enrique's Journey* (New York: Random House, 2006); Jacqueline María Hagan, *Migration Miracle: Faith, Hope, and Meaning of the Undocumented Journey* (Cambridge, MA: Harvard University Press, 2008); Tim Gaynor, *Midnight on the Line: The Secret Life of the U.S.-Mexico Border* (New York: St. Martin's Press, 2009); Miguel de la Torre, ed., *Trails of Hope and Terror: Testimonies on Immigration* (Maryknoll, NY: Orbis, 2009), 9–36; Kathryn Ferguson, Norma A. Price, and Ted Parks, *Crossing with the Virgin: Stories from the Migrant Trail* (Tucson: University of Arizona Press, 2010). Humanitarian organizations that work along the border include: Samaritans, Humane Borders, No More Deaths, and the New Sanctuary movement. These groups provide water, medical aid, and other services to undocumented immigrants. Statistics of suffering and deaths are difficult to tabulate, but see María Jiménez, *Humanitarian Crisis: Migrant Deaths at the U.S.-Mexico Border* (ACLU of San Diego and Imperial Counties and Mexico's National Commission of Human Rights, October 1, 2009); Marc R. Rosenbaum, *Border Security: Immigration Enforcement Between Ports of Entry* (Congressional Research Service, January 6, 2012). The Congressional Research Service is the public policy research arm of the US Congress. Also note the statistics at www.nomoredeaths.org.

4. Websites dedicated to gathering such accounts and other data to counter Hispanic immigration include www.immigrationshumancost.org and www.im migrationcounters.com.

5. Note Margaret Haerens, ed., *Illegal Immigration*, Opposing Viewpoints Series (Detroit: Thomson Gale, 2006); Ananda Rose, *Showdown in the Sonoran Desert: Religion, Law, and the Immigration Controversy* (New York: Oxford University Press, 2012). For periodically updated data regarding public opinion, see the Gallup website at www.gallup.com/tag/Immigration.aspx.

6. For statistics on Hispanic voting patterns in recent elections, see www .pewhispanic.org/topics/voter-participation. Immigrant organizations also try to lobby their home governments to bring pressure to bear on the US Congress regarding their status and rights. For example, Conguate (Coalición de Inmi-grantes Guatemaltecos en Estados Unidos; www.conguateus.net) strives to help Guatemalans in the US.

7. For a survey of theories, see Douglas S. Massey, Jorge Durand, and Nolan J. Malone, *Beyond Smoke and Mirrors: Mexican Immigration in an Era of Economic Integration* (New York: Russell Sage Foundation, 2002), 9–21. They discuss the models of neoclassic economics, the new economics of labor migration, segmented labor market theory, and the idea of a cumulative causation of migration. Also note Caroline B. Brettell and James F. Hollifield, eds., *Migration Theory: Talking across Disciplines*, 2nd ed. (New York: Routledge, 2008); Stephen Castles and

Mark J. Miller, *The Age of Migration: International Population Movements in the Modern World*, 4th ed. (New York: Guilford, 2009).

8. Recent extensive histories of US immigration are Timothy J. Hatton and Jeffrey G. Williamson, *Global Migration and the World Economy: Two Centuries of Policy and Performance* (Cambridge, MA: MIT Press, 2005); Aristide R. Zohlberg, *A Nation by Design: Immigration Policy in the Fashioning of America* (New York: Russell Sage Foundation; Cambridge, MA: Harvard University Press, 2007). Also see John Higham, *Strangers in the Land: Patterns of American Nativism 1860–1925*, rev. ed. (New Brunswick, NJ: Rutgers University Press, 2002). A brief survey is found in Matthew Soerens and Jenny Hwang, *Welcoming the Stranger: Justice, Compassion & Truth in the Immigration Debate* (Downers Grove, IL: InterVarsity, 2009), 45–63.

9. In addition to Hatton and Williamson, *Global Migration*; Zohlberg, *Nation by Design*; Higham, *Strangers in the Land*; see especially Jean Pfaelzer, *Driven Out: The Forgotten War against Chinese Americans* (New York: Random House, 2007); Erika Lee and Judy Yung, *Angel Island: Immigrant Gateway to America* (New York: Oxford University Press, 2010).

10. For surveys of Mexican immigration into the US, see Massey, Durand, and Malone, *Beyond Smoke and Mirrors*; Joseph Nevins, *Operation Gatekeeper: The Rise of the "Illegal Alien" and the Remaking of the U.S.-Mexico Boundary* (New York: Routledge, 2001); cf. the relevant sections in Hatton and Williamson, *Global Migration*; Zohlberg, *Nation by Design*; Higham, *Strangers in the Land*.

11. The area that is now Arizona and New Mexico was completed with the Gadsden Purchase in December 1853. For an account of this war see Timothy J. Henderson, *A Glorious Defeat: Mexico and Its War with the United States* (New York: Hill & Wang, 2007).

12. The Chicano labor leader César Chávez was prominent at this time. He organized migrant workers in California, who were predominantly Mexican-American, and was instrumental in the creation of the United Farm Workers union (UFW). Some of the activities of the UFW were aimed at eliminating competition for jobs caused by undocumented workers and preventing undocumented workers from being hired as strikebreakers. The years 1965 to 1975 were the high point of Chicano activism.

13. See especially Nevins, *Operation Gatekeeper*.

14. "Enforcing Immigration Law: The Role of State and Local Law Enforcement," Congressional Research Service, August 14, 2006, http://trac.syr.edu/immigration/library/P1072.pdf. See also the relevant sections in Zohlberg, *Nation by Design*.

15. "Judge Strikes Down Town's Immigration Law," *New York Times*, July 26, 2007, www.nytimes.com/2007/07/26/us/26cnd-hazleton.html?hp; "Hazleton Immigration Law Foes Face Uphill Battle," *Pittsburg Post-Gazette*, August 20, 2012, www.post-gazette.com/stories/business/legal/hazleton-immigration-law-foes-face-uphill-battle-649678/.

16. Sharon R. Ennis, Merarys Ríos-Vargas, and Nora G. Albert, "The Hispanic Population, 2010," 2010 Census Briefs (US Department of Commerce: US Census Bureau, May 2011); Jeffrey Passel, D'Vera Cohn, and Ana González-Barrera, "Net Migration from Mexico Falls to Zero—and Perhaps Less," Pew Hispanic Center, May 3, 2012, www.pewhispanic.org/2012/04/23/net-migration

-from-mexico-falls-to-zero-and-perhaps-less/; Jeffrey Passel and D'Vera Cohn, "Unauthorized Immigrants: 11.1 Million in 2011," December 6, 2012, www.pew hispanic.org/2012/12/06/unauthorized-immigrants-11-1-million-in-2011/.

17. Because Puerto Rico is a commonwealth of the United States, Puerto Ricans are sometimes categorized differently than the Hispanic population that has its roots in the rest of Latin America.

18. This higher birthrate among Hispanics includes those who are immigrants and those who are native-born. In both cases, the birthrate is higher than any other ethnic group. See the sources in note 16. This trend, however, has begun to see some changes. See www.nytimes.com/2013/01/01/health/us-birthrate-dips -especially-for-hispanics.html?_r=0.

19. Samuel P. Huntington, *The Clash of Civilizations and the Remaking of the World Order* (New York: Simon & Schuster, 1996); Huntington, *Who Are We? The Challenges to America's National Identity* (New York: Simon & Schuster, 2004).

20. Mark Krikorian, *The New Case against Immigration: Both Legal and Illegal* (New York: Sentinel, 2008); Victor Davis Hanson, *Mexifornia: A State of Becoming* (San Francisco: Encounter Books, 2003); Tom Tancredo, *In Mortal Danger: The Battle for America's Border and Security* (Nashville: WND Books, 2006); Patrick J. Buchanan, *State of Emergency: The Third World Invasion and Conquest of America* (New York: Thomas Dunne, 2006).

21. The most extreme, of course, are the border vigilante organizations, like the Minuteman Project, the Minuteman Civil Defense Corps, and the Patriots Coalition.

22. Linda Chávez, *Out of the Barrio: Toward a New Politics of Hispanic Assimilation* (New York: Basic Books, 1991); Chávez, "Our Hispanic Predicament," *Commentary* 105, no. 6 (1998): 47–50. A 2007 essay that generated intense reactions is "Latino Fear and Loathing," www.creators.com/opinion/linda-chavez /latino-fear-and-loathing.html. Her response to the negative feedback is "Latino Fear and Loathing, Part II," www.creators.com/opininion/linda-chavez/fear-and -loathing-part-ii.html.

23. Richard Rodríguez, *Hunger of Memory: The Education of Richard Rodriguez* (New York: Bantam, 1983); *Days of Obligation: An Argument with My Mexican Father* (New York: Penguin, 1993); *Brown: The Last Discovery of America* (New York: Penguin, 2002). An example of his biting critique of the concept is his chapter "Hispanic" in *Brown*, 103–23.

24. Rainer Muenz, "Europe: Population and Migration in 2005," Migration Policy Institute, June 1, 2006, www.migrationinformation.org/Feature/print .cfm?ID=402; Jorge Durand and Douglas S. Massey, "New World Orders: Continuity and Changes in Latin American Migration," *Annals of the American Academy of Political and Social Science* 630, no. 1 (2010): 20–52.

25. Emilio José Gómez Ciriano and Nicole Fuchs, *Inmigrante y ciudadano: Hacia una nueva cultura de la acogida* (Madrid: PPC, 2005). Also note Miguel A. Palomino, "Latino Immigration in Europe: Challenge and Opportunity for Mission," *International Bulletin for Mission Research* 28, no. 2 (2004): 55–58; Beatriz Padilla and João Peixoto, "Latin American Migration to Southern Europe," Migration Policy Institute, June 29, 2007, www.migrationinformation .org/Feature/print.cfm?ID=609; T. L. Vicente, "Latin American Immigration to

Spain," http://migrationeducation.de/48.1.html?&rid=162&cHash=96b3134cd b899a06a8ca6e12f41eafac.

26. I am using the term *assimilation* in a loose sense. For a helpful summary of the multiple ways in which immigration communities live in a new land, see Luis Rivera-Rodríguez, "Toward a Diaspora Hermeneutics (Hispanic North America)," in *Character Ethics and the Old Testament: Moral Dimensions of Scripture*, ed. M. Daniel Carroll R. and Jacqueline Lapsley (Louisville: Westminster John Knox, 2007), 169–89 (see esp. 172–76).

27. Alejandro Portes and Rubén G. Rumbaut, *Immigrant America: A Portrait*, 3rd ed. (Berkeley: University of California Press, 2006). Anthropological and sociological studies are particularly helpful. See Ann Miles, *From Cuenca to Queens: An Anthropological Story of Transnational Migration* (Austin: University of Texas Press, 2004); Jeffrey H. Cohen, *The Culture of Migration in Southern Mexico* (Austin: University of Texas Press, 2004); Robert Courtney Smith, *Mexican New York: Transnational Lives of New Immigrants* (Berkeley: University of California Press, 2006); Hannah Gill, *The Latino Migration Experience in North Carolina: New Roots in the Old North State* (Chapel Hill: University of North Carolina Press, 2010); Helen B. Marrow, *New Destination Dreaming: Immigration, Race, and Legal Status in the Rural American South* (Stanford: Stanford University Press, 2011); Steven Vertovex, "Transnationalism and Identity," *Journal of Ethnic and Migration Studies* 27, no. 4 (2001): 573–82; Peggy Levitt, "Roots and Routes: Understanding the Lives of the Second Generation Transnationally," *Journal of Ethnic and Migration Studies* 35, no. 7 (2009): 1225–42; cf. Castles and Miller, *The Age of Migration*. For diaspora studies specifically, see James Clifford, "Diasporas," in *Routes: Travel and Translation in the Late Twentieth Century* (Cambridge, MA: Harvard University Press, 1997), 244–77; Martin Baumann, "Diaspora: Genealogies of Semantics and Transcultural Comparison," *Numen* 47, no. 3 (2000): 313–37; Stéphane Dufoix, *Diasporas*, trans. W. Rodarmor (Berkeley: University of California Press, 2008). A significant element of identity affected by transnationalism is the concept of citizenship. Concern about citizenship appears in the books by Huntington, Tancredo, Buchanan, and Krikorian. It is addressed by Miles, Cohen, and Smith; note especially Portes and Rumbaut, *Immigrant America*, 117–67. The impact of economic globalization on the nation-state and citizenship also is a topic of research. Several Latin American countries allow dual citizenship, permit immigrants to vote in elections, and provide services to émigrés. Membership within a society vis-à-vis outsiders is discussed in legal ethics as well. See, for example, Michael Waltzer, *Spheres of Justice: A Defense of Pluralism and Equality* (New York: Basic Books, 1983), 31–63; William James Booth, "Foreigners: Insiders, Outsiders, and the Ethics of Membership," *Review of Politics* 59, no. 2 (1997): 259–92; William R. O'Neill and William C. Spohn, "Rights of Passage: The Ethics of Immigration and Refugee Policy," *Theological Studies* 59, no. 1 (1998): 84–106.

28. In addition to the sources cited in the previous note, see Jack Citrin et al., "Testing Huntington: Is Hispanic Immigration a Threat to American Identity?," *Perspectives on Politics* 5, no. 1 (2007): 31–48; Roger Waldinger, "Between Here and There: How Attached Are Latinos to Their Native Country?" Pew Hispanic Center, October 25, 2007, www.pewhispanic.org/reports/report.php?ReportID=80; Paul Taylor et al., "When Labels Don't Fit: Hispanics and Their Views of Identity,"

Pew Hispanic Center, April 4, 2012, www.pewhispanic.org/2012/04/04/when-labels
-dont-fit-hispanics-and-their-views-of-identity/. Note the helpful ethnic identity/
assimilation grids in Orlando Crespo, *Being Latino in Christ: Finding Wholeness
in Your Ethnic Identity* (Downers Grove, IL: InterVarsity, 2003), 40–53.

29. There are many other writers, of course, but these are ones I have read:
Francisco Goldman, *The Long Night of White Chickens* (New York: Atlantic
Monthly, 1992) and *The Ordinary Seaman* (New York: Atlantic Monthly, 1997);
Sandra Cisneros, *Caramelo or Puro Cuento* (New York: Vintage, 2002); Victor
Villaseñor, *Burro Genius: A Memoir* (New York: HarperCollins, 2004); Edmundo
Paz Soldán, *The Matter of Desire*, trans. Lisa Carter (Boston: Houghton Mifflin,
2001); Julia Álvarez, *How the García Girls Lost Their Accent* (New York: Plume,
1992) and *Once upon a Quinceañera: Coming of Age in the U.S.A.* (New York:
Viking, 2007). Cf. Mark Griffin and Theron Walker, *Living on the Borders: What the
Church Can Learn from Ethnic Immigrant Cultures* (Grand Rapids: Brazos, 2004).

30. Cisneros, *Caramelo or Puro Cuento*, 434.

31. Issues of identity and *mestizaje* have been a source of theological reflection
among Hispanic theologians as well, but that discussion is reserved for the next
chapter. Another term that should be mentioned is *mulatez*. It refers to the cultural
mix with the African (a *mulatto* is a dark-skinned person). For simplicity's sake,
I will limit myself to *mestizaje*.

32. See the comments of Carlos Fuentes, *The Buried Mirror: Reflections on
Spain and the New World* (London: André Deutsch, 1992), 341–55.

33. Huntington prefers the metaphor of tomato soup, in which new elements
are added, "enriching the taste, but not significantly altering the substance" (*Who
Are We?*, 184). A richer appreciation of the melting-pot idea, more optimistic and
celebratory of difference, is found in Michael Barone, *The New Americans: How
the Melting Pot Can Work Again* (Washington, DC: Regnery, 2001).

34. Tancredo, *In Mortal Danger*, 155–72.

35. In a March 2012 report the Inter-American Development Bank reported
that in 2011 $61 billion was sent in remittances to Latin America and the Carib-
bean, of which about 75 percent came from the US: "Remittances to Latin America and the Caribbean rose to $61 billion in 2011," www.iadb.org/en/news/news
-releases/2012-03-08/report-remittances-to-latin-america-rose-in-2011,9899.html.

36. Studies can be found on their respective websites: www.cis.org; www.fairus
.org; www.heritage.org/issues/immigration.

37. See Gordon H. Hanson, *Why Does Immigration Divide America? Public
Finance and Political Opposition to Open Borders* (Washington, DC: Institute for
International Economics, 2005), 27–40.

38. For example, ibid.; George J. Borjas, ed., *Mexican Immigration to the
United States, National Bureau of Economic Research Conference Report* (Chicago: University of Chicago Press, 2007); Krikorian, *The New Case against Immigration*, 212–35.

39. Lant Pritchett, *Let Their People Come: Breaking the Gridlock on Global
Mobility* (Washington, DC: Center for Global Development, 2006); David Bacon,
Illegal People: How Globalization Creates Migration and Criminalizes Immigrants
(Boston: Beacon, 2008); Jason L. Riley, *Let Them In: The Case for Open Borders*
(New York: Gotham, 2010). From a conservative viewpoint, see Jeb Bush and Clint
Bolick, *Immigration Wars: Forging an American Solution* (New York: Threshold

Editions, 2013). For various studies dealing specifically with Hispanic immigrants, see www.pewhispanic.org/topics/economics-and-personal-finances. For portrayals of working conditions of the undocumented, which should figure in to these discussions, see Bacon, *Illegal People*; Southern Poverty Law Center, *Under Siege: Life for Low-Income Latinos in the South* (Montgomery: SPLC, 2009); Gabriel Thompson, *Working in the Shadows: A Year of Doing Jobs (Most) Americans Won't Do* (New York: Nation Books, 2010).

40. Inter-American Development Bank, "Remittances." For what follows regarding the impact of emigration in Guatemala, see Silvia Irene, ed., *Después de Nuestro Señor, Estados Unidos: Perspectivas de análisis del comportamiento e implicaciones de la migración internacional en Guatemala* (Guatemala: FLACSO, 2004); David Stoll, "El debate migratorio en los Estados Unidos como contienda entre cuatro distintas versiones del sueño norteamericano," presented at the monthly meeting of La Sociedad Evangélica de Estudios Socio-religiosos, Guatemala City, July 4, 2007. My example is Guatemala, but there is research on other places, such as Cuenca, Bolivia (Miles, *From Cuenca to Queens*); Oaxaca, Mexico (Smith, *Mexican New York*; Cohen, *Culture of Migration in Southern Mexico*; Leah K. VanWey, Catherine M. Tucker, and Eileen Diaz McConnell, "Community Organization, Migration, and Remittances in Oaxaca," *Latin American Research Review* 40, no. 1 [2005]: 83–107); Jalisco, Mexico (David Fitzgerald, *A Nation of Emigrants: How Mexico Manages Its Migration* [Berkeley: University of California Press, 2009]).

41. See the information provided by the United Nations at http://unstats.un.org/unsd/demographic/sconcerns/migration/. For economic globalization and the migration of labor (although these sources do not all take the same point of view), see Pritchett, *Let Their People Come*; Bacon, *Illegal People*; Jagdish Bhagwati, *In Defense of Globalization* (New York: Oxford University Press, 2004); Joseph E. Stiglitz and Andrew Charlton, *Fair Trade for All: How Trade Can Promote Development* (New York: Oxford University Press, 2005); Brettell and Hollifield, *Migration Theory*; cf. M. Daniel Carroll R., "The Challenge of Economic Globalization for Theology: From Latin America to a Hermeneutics of Responsibility," in *Globalizing Theology: Christian Belief and Practice in an Era of World Christianity*, ed. C. Ott and H. Netland (Grand Rapids: Baker Academic, 2006), 199–212.

42. Thomas L. Friedman's analysis of Mexico in the new global market in *The World Is Flat: A Brief History of the Twenty-First Century* (New York: Farrar, Straus and Giroux, 2005) speaks of government bureaucracy, cultural patterns, and the imperative to change its vision and ways of operating its economy, but nowhere does he mention the human cost or labor migration as consequences of Mexico's situation (pp. 309–36). For a spirited defense of Mexico's journey into the global economy, see Vicente Fox with Rob Allyn, *Revolution of Hope: The Life, Faith, and Dreams of a Mexican President* (New York: Viking, 2007).

43. "Changing Faiths: Latinos and the Transformation of American Religion," Pew Hispanic Center, April 25, 2007, www.pewhispanic.org/reports/report.php?ReportID=75; "When Labels Don't Fit: Hispanics and Their Views of Identity," Pew Hispanic Center, April 4, 2012, www.pewhispanic.org/2012/04/04/v-politics-values-and-religion/.

44. Virgilio Elizondo, *Galilean Journey: The Mexican-American Promise* (Maryknoll, NY: Orbis, 1983), 32–48; Orlando O. Espín, *The Faith of the People: Theological Reflections on Popular Catholicism* (Maryknoll, NY: Orbis, 1997);

David A. Badillo, *Latinos and the New Immigrant Church* (Baltimore: Johns Hopkins University Press, 2006); Nestor Medina, *Mestizaje: Remapping Race, Culture, and Faith in Latina/o Catholicism*, Studies in Latino/a Catholicism (Maryknoll, NY: Orbis, 2009); Timothy Matovina, *Latino Catholicism: Transformation in America's Largest Church* (Princeton: Princeton University Press, 2011); cf. Edwin David Aponte, *¡Santo! Varieties of Latina/o Spirituality* (Maryknoll, NY: Orbis, 2012). Other grassroots beliefs include appeals to Saint (Father) Toribio Romo (Ben Daniel, *Neighbor: Christian Encounters with "Illegal" Immigration* [Louisville: Westminster John Knox, 2010], 3–12) and the bizarre Santa Muerte (R. Andrew Chestnut, *Devoted to Death: Santa Muerte, the Skeleton Saint* [New York: Oxford University Press, 2012]).

45. For helpful introductions to Hispanic Pentecostalism, see Samuel Solivan, *The Spirit, Pathos and Liberation: Toward an Hispanic Pentecostal Theology*, Journal of Pentecostal Theology Supplements Series 14 (Sheffield: Sheffield Academic Press, 1998); Arlene M. Sánchez Walsh, *Latino Pentecostal Identity: Evangelical Faith, Self, and Society*, Religion and American Culture Series (New York: Columbia University Press, 2003). For broader discussions of Hispanic Protestantism, see David Maldonado, ed., *Protestantes/Protestants: Hispanic Christianity within Mainline Traditions* (Nashville: Abingdon, 1999); the pertinent chapters in Edwin David Aponte and Miguel A. de la Torre, eds., *Handbook of Latino/a Theologies* (St. Louis: Chalice, 2006); Juan F. Martínez, *Los Protestantes: An Introduction to Latino Protestantism in the United States* (Santa Barbara: Praeger, 2011).

46. Gastón Espinosa, Virgilio Elizondo, and Jesse Miranda, *Latino Religions and Civic Activism in the United States* (New York: Oxford University Press, 2005); "Immigrant-Led Organizers in Their Own Voices: Local Realities and Shared Visions," Catholic Legal Immigration Network, May 2006, www.cliniclegal.org /Publications/Freepublications/CLINIC_Reportonorganizers_final.pdf; cf. Pew Hispanic Center, "Changing Faiths."

47. Crespo, *Being Latino in Christ*; Juan Francisco Martínez, *Walk with the People: Latino Ministry in the United States* (Nashville: Abingdon, 2008); Martínez, *Los Protestantes*; Daniel A. Rodríguez, *A Future for the Latino Church: Models for Multilingual, Multigenerational Hispanic Congregations* (Downers Grove, IL: InterVarsity, 2011).

48. Philip Jenkins, *The Next Christendom: The Coming of Global Christianity*, 3rd ed. (New York: Oxford University Press, 2011). Note the annual statistical table published in *International Bulletin of Mission Research* and the data available from the Center for the Study of Global Christianity at Gordon-Conwell Theological Seminary (www.gordonconwell.edu/resources/CSGC-Resources.cfm).

49. Philip Jenkins, *The New Faces of Christianity: Believing the Bible in the Global South* (New York: Oxford University Press, 2006).

50. During the era of the Cold War, the label *Third World* referred to those countries not in Western Europe and North America (the First World) or in the Soviet Union (the Second World). The term *Two-Thirds World* arose after the demise of the Soviet Union as a description for the part of the globe that held two-thirds of the planet's population and landmass. Today the labels *Two-Thirds World* and *Majority World* occasionally are applied also to minority groups in Western Europe and the US.

51. Jehu Hanciles, *Beyond Christendom: Globalization, African Migration, and the Transformation of the West* (Maryknoll, NY: Orbis, 2008); S. Hun Kim and Wonsuk Ma, ed., *Korean Diaspora and Christian Mission*, Regnum Studies in Mission (Eugene, OR: Wipf & Stock, 2011); Enoch Wan, *Diaspora Missiology: Theory, Methodology, and Practice* (Portland, OR: Institute of Diaspora Studies, 2011); J. D. Payne, *Strangers Next Door: Immigration, Migration, and Mission* (Downers Grove, IL: InterVarsity, 2012). Also note the publications of the Lausanne Committee for World Evangelization (LCWE): Lausanne Committee for World Evangelization, *The New People Next Door* (Lausanne Occasional Paper 55 [2004], www.lausanne.org/en/documents/lops/871-lop-55.html); *Scattered to Gather: Embracing the Global Trend of Diaspora* (Manila: LifeChange Publishing, 2010).

Chapter 2: Of Immigrants, Refugees, and Exiles

1. Scholarly resources are mentioned in the endnotes for those who might desire to pursue details in greater depth. I have kept these to a minimum because of the more popular focus of this book. I will be dealing with the canonical shape of these texts instead of with scholarly reconstructions. For a discussion of such matters, see my "Ethics and Old Testament Interpretation," in *Hearing the Old Testament: Listening for God's Address*, ed. C. G. Bartholomew and J. H. Beldman (Grand Rapids: Eerdmans, 2012), 204–27.

2. There is a huge amount of material by Hispanic scholars regarding the importance of reading the Bible with an explicitly Hispanic lens. This is an important point that I affirm, but the confines of this book do not permit an exploration of that hermeneutical discussion. See the appendix for sources that address this issue and notes 10 and 30 below. It also is worthwhile to distinguish between what scholars might argue are essential ingredients for a Hispanic approach to the biblical text and the jargon that is utilized in those proposals and what actually goes on among Hispanic laypeople and in Hispanic churches. The focus there often is on personal and familial needs or largely is influenced, for example, by certain Pentecostal themes. Societal issues usually remain in the background, except as they immediately affect church members. The importance of distinguishing academic discourse of Minority or Majority World groups from that of the "common people" is addressed directly by Jenkins in *The New Faces of Christianity*.

3. See Conferencia del Episcopado Mexicano and the United States Conference of Catholic Bishops, *Strangers No Longer: Together on the Journey of Hope* (Washington, DC: United States Conference of Catholic Bishops, 2003), www.nccbuscc.org/mrs/stranger.htm; cf. William R. O'Neill and William C. Spohn, "Rights of Passage: The Ethics of Immigration and Refugee Policy," *Theological Studies* 59, no. 1 (1998): 84–106; Andrew M. Yuengert, *Inhabiting the Land: The Case for the Right to Migrate*, Christian Social Thought Series 6 (Grand Rapids: Acton Institute, 2003), 11–18. Pope John Paul II's "Migration Day" messages are available on the Vatican website (www.vatican.va); cf. Pope Benedict XVI, *Charity in Truth/Caritas in Veritae* (San Francisco: Ignatius, 2009), 127–29. For CELAM, visit www.celam.org.

4. For a systematic theology view, see Gordon R. Lewis and Bruce A. Demarest, *Integrative Theology*, 3 vols. (Grand Rapids: Zondervan, 1990), 2:123–80. For a biblical theology perspective, see J. Richard Middleton, *The Liberating Image:*

The Imago Dei *in Genesis 1* (Grand Rapids: Brazos, 2005); cf. Christopher J. H. Wright, *Old Testament Ethics for the People of God* (Downers Grove, IL: Inter-Varsity, 2004), 116–29; Wright, *The Mission of God: Unlocking the Bible's Grand Narrative* (Downers Grove, IL: InterVarsity, 2007), 421–28.

5. O'Neill and Spohn, "Rights of Passage," 91–97; "Convention on the Protection of the Rights of All Migrant Workers and Members of Their Families," UN Office of the High Commission for Human Rights (1990), www.unhchr.ch/html /menu3/b/m_mwctoc.htm.

6. Early theological reflections on *mestizaje* are Elizondo, *Galilean Journey*; Justo L. González, *Santa Biblia: The Bible through Hispanic Eyes* (Nashville: Abingdon, 1996), 77–90. At a very personal level note Crespo, *Being Latino in Christ*. Recent discussions of the complexity of the concept and its challenges include Medina, *Mestizaje*; Carmen Nanko-Fernández, *Theologizing in Spanglish: Context, Community, and Ministry*, Studies in Latino/a Catholicism (Maryknoll, NY: Orbis, 2010).

7. Each of the items in this list has pastoral concerns as its root. For example, in terms of family issues: immigrants who have left spouses and children in their home country and have another family or partner in the US, the incidence of alcoholism and drug use, the allure of gangs for young people, the temptation of irresponsible consumerism after coming from a more deprived background.

8. In this book I will use the term *sojourner* instead of another valid translation option, *resident alien*. In today's climate, there may be some controversial connotations attached to *resident* and *alien*. *Sojourner* is a more neutral label.

9. James K. Hoffmeier, *Israel in Egypt: The Evidence for the Authenticity of the Exodus Tradition* (New York: Oxford University Press, 1996), 52–76; Hoffmeier, *The Immigration Crisis: Immigrants, Aliens, and the Bible* (Wheaton: Crossway, 2009), 43–45.

10. Jean-Pierre Ruiz, *Readings from the Edges: The Bible and People on the Move* (Maryknoll, NY: Orbis, 2011), 64–68; M. Daniel Carroll R., "Reading the Bible through Other Lenses: New Vistas from a Hispanic Diaspora Perspective," in *Global Voices: Reading the Bible in the Majority World*, ed. C. S. Keener and M. D. Carroll R. (Peabody, MA: Hendrickson, 2012), 17–19.

11. For discussions on redemption of property and the debate about whether levirate marriage is in view, see Robert L. Hubbard Jr., *Ruth*, New International Commentary on the Old Testament (Grand Rapids: Eerdmans, 1988), 48–63; Tamara Cohn Eskanazi and Tikva Frymer-Kensky, *Ruth*, JPS Bible Commentary (Philadelphia: Jewish Publication Society, 2011), xxviii–xxxviii, liii–lv. For the theology, see Hubbard, *Ruth*, 66–74; Eskanazi and Frymer-Kensky, *Ruth*, xlviii–lv; Charles Halton, "An Indecent Proposal: The Theological Core of the Book of Ruth," *Scandinavian Journal of the Old Testament* 26, no. 1 (2012): 30–43.

12. Dianne Bergant, "Ruth: The Migrant Who Saved the People," in *Migration, Religious Experience, and Globalization*, ed. G. Campese and P. Ciallella (New York: Center for Migration Studies, 2003), 49–61; Neil Glover, "Your People, My People: An Exploration of Ethnicity in Ruth," *Journal for the Study of the Old Testament* 33, no. 3 (2009): 293–313; Gale A. Yee, "'She Stood in Tears amid the Alien Corn': Ruth, the Perpetual Foreigner and Model Minority," in *They Were All Together in One Place? Toward Minority Biblical Criticism*, ed. R. C. Bailey, T. B. Liew, and F. F. Segovia, Semeia 57 (Atlanta: Society of Biblical Literature, 2009),

119–40. Also note the lay lessons by Diane Levy Jacobson and David Vásquez Levy, *Ruth*, Books of Faith (Minneapolis: Augsburg Fortress, 2012).

13. Note Richard Alba and Victor Nee, "Assimilation," in *The New Americans: A Guide to Immigration Since 1965*, ed. M. C. Waters and R. Ueda (Cambridge, MA: Harvard University Press, 2007), 124–36; cf. Carroll R., "Reading the Bible through Other Lenses," 20–22. Other readings of Ruth using social sciences include Bonnie Honig, "Ruth, the Model Emigrée: Mourning and the Symbolic Politics of Immigration," *Political Theory* 25, no. 1 (1997): 112–36; Victor H. Matthews, "The Determination of Social Identity in the Story of Ruth," in *The Family in Life and in Death: The Family in Ancient Israel—Sociological and Archaeological Perspectives*, ed. P. Dutcher-Walls, Library of Biblical Studies/Old Testament Studies 504 (New York: T&T Clark, 2009), 16–27; Glover, "Your People, My People."

14. Anthony Leahy, "Ethnic Diversity in Ancient Egypt," in *Civilizations of the Ancient Near East*, ed. Jack M. Sasson, 4 vols. (Peabody, MA: Hendrickson, 1995), 1:225–34; Edda Bresciani, "Foreigners," in *The Egyptians*, ed. S. Donadoni (Chicago: University of Chicago Press, 1997), 221–53; Hoffmeier, *Israel in Egypt*, 77–106; K. A. Kitchen, *On the Reliability of the Old Testament* (Grand Rapids: Eerdmans, 2003), 343–52. For changing Egyptian views toward peoples outside Egypt, see Kenton L. Sparks, *Ethnicity and Identity in Ancient Israel: Prolegomena to the Study of Ethnic Sentiments and Their Expression in the Hebrew Bible* (Winona Lake, IN: Eisenbrauns, 1998), 75–93.

15. For the debate about this population increase, see Israel Finkelstein, "The Settlement History of Jerusalem in the Eighth and Seventh Centuries BC," *Revue Biblique* 115, no. 4 (2008): 499–515. I do not subscribe to all of Finkelstein's historical reconstruction. Also see Aaron A. Burke, "An Anthropological Model for the Investigation of Refugees in Iron Age Judah and Its Environs," in *Interpreting Exile: Displacement and Deportation in Biblical and Modern Contexts*, ed. B. E. Kelle, R. Ames, and J. L. Wright, Ancient Israel and Its Literature (Atlanta: Society of Biblical Literature, 2011), 41–56.

16. The text of Sennacherib's account of his third campaign, of which the siege of Jerusalem was a part, is found in *The Context of Scripture*, ed. W. H. Hallo and K. L. Younger Jr., 3 vols. (Leiden: Brill, 2000), 2:302–3.

17. For a broader discussion, which includes biblical accounts, see Daniel C. Snell, *Flight and Freedom in the Ancient Near East*, Culture and History of the Ancient Near East 8 (Leiden: Brill, 2001).

18. Hoffmeier, *Israel in Egypt*, 138–44.

19. Ibid., 109–22.

20. Bustaney Oded, *Mass Deportations and Deportees in the Neo-Assyrian Empire* (Weisbaden: Dr. Ludwig Reichert Verlag, 1979), 75–115; Oded, "The Settlements of the Israelite and the Judean Exiles in Mesopotamia in the 8th–6th Centuries BCE," in *Studies in Historical Geography and Biblical Historiography Presented to Zecharia Kallai*, ed. G. Galil and M. Weinfeld, Supplements to Vetus Testamentum 452 (Leiden: Brill, 2000), 91–103; K. Lawson Younger Jr., "'Give Us Our Daily Bread': Everyday Life for the Israelite Deportees," in *Life and Culture in the Ancient Near East*, ed. R. E. Averbeck, M. W. Chavalas, and D. B. Weisberg (Bethesda, MD: CDL Press, 2003), 269–88. Also note various articles in K. Van Lerberghe and A. Schoors, eds., *Immigration and Emigration within the Ancient*

Near East: Festschrift E. Lipiński, Orientalia Lovaniensia Analecta 65 (Leuven: Uitgeverij Peeters en Departement Oriëntalistiek, 1995).

21. In addition to the biblical text, note Laurie E. Pearce, "New Evidence for Judeans in Babylonia," in *Judah and the Judeans in the Persian Period*, ed. Oded Lipschits and Manfred Oeming (Winona Lake, IN: Eisenbrauns, 2006), 399–411; W. G. Lambert, "A Document from a Community of Exiles in Babylonia," in *New Seals and Inscriptions, Hebrew, Idumean, and Cuneiform*, ed. M. Lubetski, Hebrew Bible Monographs 8 (Sheffield: Sheffield Phoenix, 2007), 201–5; Kathleen Abraham, "An Inheritance Division among Judeans in Babylonia from the Early Persian Period," in Lubetski, *New Seals and Inscriptions*, 206–21; Daniel L. Smith-Christopher, *A Biblical Theology of Exile* (Minneapolis: Fortress, 2002). Also see the sources in the preceding note.

22. Daniel L. Smith-Christopher has applied refugee, trauma, and diaspora studies to the exile in *The Religion of the Landless: The Social Context of the Exile* (Bloomington, IN: Meyer-Stone, 1989) and *A Biblical Theology of Exile*; cf. Smith-Christopher, "Reading War and Trauma: Suggestions Toward a Social-Psychological Exegesis of Exile and War in Biblical Texts," in *Interpreting Exile*, 253–74. People in these situations demonstrate several characteristics listed in this paragraph.

23. Katherine E. Southwood has reflected on the intermarriage scenario in Ezra within the framework of ethnicity and return migration studies in several publications, most recently in *Ethnicity and the Mixed Marriage Crisis in Ezra 9–10: An Anthropological Approach*, Oxford Theological Monographs (Oxford: Oxford University Press, 2012). Other debated details include how large of a group did these measures actually affect and how the leaders of the returnees were handling the theological and biblical bases of their decisions (e.g., the awareness and treatment of Deut. 23:2–8).

24. Gregory Lee Cuéllar connects these texts in Isaiah (which he dates to the postexilic period) to the experience of Mexican immigrants in *Voices of Marginality: Exile and Return in Second Isaiah 40–55 and the Mexican Immigrant Experience*, American University Studies, Series VII, vol. 271 (New York: Peter Lang, 2008).

25. Scholars have attempted to identify the possible conflicts between the returnees and those who had remained in the land, such as those mentioned in this paragraph. See the sources in notes 22 and 23 above. For other technical discussions, see Oded Lipschits, Gary N. Knoppers, and Manfred Oeming, eds., *Judah and the Judeans in the Achaemenid Period: Negotiating Identity in an International Context* (Winona Lake, IN: Eisenbrauns, 2011); Megan Bishop Moore and Brad E. Kelle, *Biblical History and Israel's Past: The Changing Study of the Bible and History* (Grand Rapids: Eerdmans, 2011), 396–464.

26. For life and politics in the Persian Empire, see Pierre Briant, *From Cyrus to Alexander: A History of the Persian Empire*, trans. P. T. Daniels (Winona Lake, IN: Eisenbrauns, 2002).

27. For these and other issues, see Karen Jobes, *Esther*, NIV Application Commentary (Grand Rapids: Zondervan, 1999), and Adele Berlin, *Esther*, JPS Bible Commentary (Philadelphia: Jewish Publication Society, 2001). For more details on the gate and women in the palace, see Briant, *From Cyrus to Alexander*, 259–61 and 277–86, respectively.

28. Esther is the only book of the Bible that does not mention God. This caused some ancients to doubt whether it should be included in the canon. The Septuagint, which is the Greek translation of the Hebrew text, resolved the problem by adding over one hundred lines to the book. The additions include prayers and the insertion of the name of God.

29. Jacob Neusner, "Babylonia," *Encyclopaedia Judaica*, 2nd ed. (Detroit: Macmillan, 2007), 3:24–30; Nissim Kazzaz, "Iraq," *Encyclopaedia Judaica*, 10:14–21.

30. In addition to the sources in supra note 10, see Luis Rivera-Rodríguez, "Toward a Diaspora Hermeneutics (Hispanic North America)"; Carroll R., "Reading the Bible through Other Lenses." Also see Fernando F. Segovia, "In the World but Not of It: Exile as a Locus for a Theology of the Diaspora," in Isasi-Díaz and Segovia, *Hispanic/Latino Theology*, 195–217; González, *Santa Biblia*, 91–102; Ada María Isasi-Díaz, "'By the Rivers of Babylon': Exile as a Way of Life," in *Reading from This Place: Social Location and Biblical Interpretation in Global Perspective*, ed. Fernando Segovia and Mary Ann Tolbert (Minneapolis: Fortress, 1995), 149–63; cf. Bob Ekblad, *Reading the Bible with the Damned* (Louisville: Westminster John Knox, 2005), 113–26.

31. This is also the title of a book by Eldin Villafañe, *Seek the Peace of the City: Reflections on Urban Ministry* (Grand Rapids: Eerdmans, 1995).

32. Hans de Wit, *En la dispersión, el texto es patria: Introducción a la hermenéutica clásica, moderna y posmoderna* (San José, Costa Rica: Universidad Bíblica Latinoamericana, 2002).

Chapter 3: The Law and the Sojourner

1. Buchanan, *State of Emergency*, 220–25.

2. Philip J. King and Lawrence E. Stager, *Life in Biblical Israel*, Library of Ancient Israel (Louisville: Westminster John Knox, 2001), 61–63; cf. Victor H. Matthews and Don C. Benjamin, *Social World of Ancient Israel, 1250–587 BCE* (Peabody, MA: Hendrickson, 1993), 82–95; Andrew Arterbury, *Entertaining Angels: Early Christian Hospitality in Its Mediterranean Setting*, New Testament Monographs 8 (Sheffield: Sheffield Phoenix Press, 2005), 55–93, and passim.

3. Wright, *Old Testament Ethics for the People of God*, 68. His full discussion appears on pp. 48–75, 182–211. For Deut. 4:5–8, see Wright, *Mission of God*, 378–80; cf. Daniel I. Block, "The Privilege of Calling: The Mosaic Pattern for Missions," in Block, *How I Love Your Torah, O Lord! Studies in the Book of Deuteronomy* (Eugene: Cascade, 2011), 140–61.

4. One debate among scholars who study Old Testament law is whether the shared vocabulary and ideas of these law codes suggest that they stem from a shared Mesopotamian legal tradition.

5. Moshe Weinfeld, *Social Justice in Ancient Israel and in the Ancient Near East* (Minneapolis: Fortress; Jerusalem: Magnes, 1995); J. Gordon McConville, *God and Earthly Power: An Old Testament Political Theology, Genesis–Kings*, Library of Hebrew Bible/Old Testament Studies 454 (London: T&T Clark, 2007); cf. Peter T. Vogt, *Deuteronomic Theology and the Significance of Torah: A Reappraisal* (Winona Lake, IN: Eisenbrauns, 2006).

6. The key figure here is Clifford Geertz. Note his "Local Knowledge: Fact and Law in Comparative Perspective," in *Local Knowledge: Further Essays in*

Interpretive Anthropology (New York: Basic Books, 1983), 167–234; and "Off Echoes: Some Comments on Anthropology and Law," *Political and Legal Anthropology Review* 19, no. 2 (1996): 33–37.

7. See, e.g., Mario Liverani, *International Relations in the Ancient Near East, 1600–1100 BC*, Studies in Diplomacy (New York: Palgrave, 2001), 46–76; Snell, *Flight and Freedom in the Ancient Near East*. Attitudes to outsiders could be quite negative. Note the language used by Mesopotamian sources of the Gutians and the Amorites. See Jerrold S. Cooper, *The Curse of Agade* (Baltimore: Johns Hopkins University Press, 1983), 30–36; for Egyptian prejudices and measures, see chapter 2, notes 9 and 14. For a broader discussion of the complex engagement with foreigners in the ancient world, see Erich S. Gruen, *Rethinking the Other in Antiquity* (Princeton: Princeton University Press, 2011).

8. D. I. Block, "Sojourner," *International Standard Bible Encyclopaedia*, ed. G. W. Bromiley, rev. ed. (Grand Rapids: Eerdmans, 1988), 4:561–64; R. J. D. Knauth, "Alien, Foreign Resident," *Dictionary of the Old Testament: Pentateuch*, ed. T. D. Alexander and D. W. Baker (Downers Grove, IL: InterVarsity, 2003), 26–33. Several authors try to reconstruct a historical development of views and terminology regarding foreigners in ancient Israel. See D. Kellermann, *"gûr," Theological Dictionary of the Old Testament*, ed. G. J. Botterweck and H. Ringgren (Grand Rapids: Eerdmans, 1975), 2:439–49; Christiana van Houten, *The Alien in Israelite Law*, Journal for the Study of the Old Testament Supplement Series 107 (Sheffield: Sheffield Academic Press, 1991); José E. Ramírez Kidd, *Alterity and Identity in Israel: The Ger in the Old Testament*, Beihefte zur Zeitschrift für die alttestamentliche Wissenschaft 283 (Berlin: de Gruyter, 1999); and various chapters in *The Foreigner and the Law: Perspectives from the Hebrew Bible and the Ancient Near East*, ed. R. Achenbach, R. Albertz, and J. Wöhle, Beihefte zur Zeitschrift fuur Altorientalische und Biblische Rechtsgeschichte 16 (Wiesbaden: Harrassowitz, 2011). Also see below, note 17.

9. There are exceptions to this generalization, of course. *Zār* can refer to lay Israelites who are not Levites (Exod. 29:33; Lev. 22:10–13; Num. 1:51; 3:10, 38); they are "foreign" in the sense that they are not qualified to do what only the priests can perform.

10. *Nokrî/nēkār*: other gods (Josh. 24:20; 1 Sam. 7:3; Jer. 5:19; Mal. 2:11), followers of other gods (Ezek. 44:7–9), the licentious woman (Prov. 6:24; 23:27), or foreign women (1 Kings 11:1; Ezra 10:2; Neh. 13:26). *Zār*: enemies (Ps. 54:3 [54:5 MT]; Isa. 1:7; 29:5), foreign gods (Deut. 32:16; Jer. 2:25), an adulterous woman (Prov. 22:14). These two terms can appear in parallel, referring to, for example, an immoral woman (Prov. 2:16; 5:20; 7:5) or enemies (Obad. 11). They also occur together when they refer to different things as "foreign" (Jer. 5:19). These are selected verses. The terms appear in many other passages.

11. In passages such as Prov. 6:1 and 11:15 there is a question whether the "stranger" is an individual who is not well known or a literal foreigner. If the latter, then these passages are a warning not to do business with these foreigners.

12. 1 Chron. 29:15 and Ps. 39:12 [39:13 MT] have this pairing, too, but in reference to the experience of Israelites.

13. The focus here is primarily on the noun *gēr*. It occurs over ninety times in the Old Testament. Its verbal root, *gûr* I, appears eighty-one times and is usually translated as "sojourn" or "live."

14. Even with these distinctions, there is never the negative reaction to *gēr* that one encounters with *nokrî* and *zār*. The clearest example of this difference in response is found in the fact that the passages that condemn intermarriage in Ezra (chaps. 9–10) and Nehemiah (chap. 13) use *nokrî* and *zār*, never *gēr*, to refer to the women rejected by Israel's leaders.

15. Ramírez Kidd, *Alterity and Identity in Israel*, 110–16; cf. the sources above in note 20 of chapter 2.

16. For the Laws of Eshnunna and Hammurabi, see Hallo, *Context of Scripture*, 2:332–35 and 335–53, respectively.

17. In addition to the sources in note 8 of this chapter, see F. A. Spina, "Israelites as *gerim*: Sojourners in Social and Historical Context," in *The Word of the Lord Shall Go Forth: Essays in Honor of David Noel Freedman in Celebration of His Sixtieth Birthday*, ed. C. L. Meyers and M. O'Connor, 321–35 (Winona Lake, IN: Eisenbrauns, 1983), 321–35; Donald E. Gowan, "Wealth and Poverty in the Old Testament: The Case of the Widow, the Orphan, and the Sojourner," *Interpretation* 41, no. 4 (1987): 341–53; R. Rendtorff, "The *Ger* in the Priestly Laws of the Pentateuch," in *Ethnicity and the Bible*, ed. Mark G. Brett, Biblical Interpretation Series (Leiden: Brill, 1996), 77–87; Patrick D. Miller, "Israel as Host to Strangers," in *Israelite Religion and Biblical Theology: Collected Essays*, ed. Patrick D. Miller, Journal for the Study of the Old Testament Supplement Series 267 (Sheffield: Sheffield Academic Press, 2000), 548–71.

18. Levites are sometimes included in these measures, because in the law they are not able to own property (Deut. 14:27–29; 16:11, 14; 26:12–13). The verb *gûr* I is applied to them (they "sojourn" in the land, Deut. 18:6), but the noun *gēr* never is.

19. For a fuller discussion of Deuteronomy, see M. Daniel Carroll R., "Welcoming the Stranger: Toward a Theology of Immigration in Deuteronomy," in *For Our Good Always: Studies on the Message and Influence of Deuteronomy in Honor of Daniel I. Block*, ed. J. S. DeRouchie, J. Gile, and K. J. Turner (Winona Lake, IN: Eisenbrauns, 2013), 441–61.

20. Exod. 12:19, 49; Lev. 16:29; 17:15; 18:26; 19:34; 24:16, 22; Num. 9:14; 15:29–30; cf. Lev. 19:34; 25:35.

21. For wonderful discussions of foreigners within Israel, see J. Daniel Hays, *From Every People and Nation: A Biblical Theology of Race*, New Studies in Biblical Theology 14 (Leicester: Apollos; Downers Grove, IL: InterVarsity, 2003).

22. *Nokrî* also occurs in Isa. 60:10 and 61:5 (along with *zār*). These passages speak of the judgment on the nations who had cruelly oppressed the people of God. Here, the negative connotation of "foreign" reappears.

23. This is the contention of Hoffmeier, *The Immigration Crisis*, who links legal foreign resident immigrants with the *gēr*, and the undocumented foreigner with *nokrî* and *zār*.

Chapter 4: Welcoming the Stranger

1. See, for example, Craig A. Evans, *Fabricating Jesus: How Modern Scholars Distort the Gospels* (Downers Grove, IL: InterVarsity, 2006); Richard Bauckham, *Jesus and the Eyewitnesses: The Gospels as Eyewitness Testimony* (Grand Rapids: Eerdmans, 2006).

2. Craig S. Keener, *A Commentary on the Gospel of Matthew* (Grand Rapids: Eerdmans, 1999), 110–11 (see his excursus on the magi on p. 99); cf. Darrell L. Bock and Gregory J. Herrick, *Jesus in Context: Background Readings for Gospel Study* (Grand Rapids: Baker Academic, 2005), 52–54.

3. Craig L. Blomberg, *Jesus and the Gospels: An Introduction and Survey*, 2nd ed. (Nashville: B&H Academic, 2009), 8–86; Eckhard J. Schnabel, *Early Christian Mission*, vol. 1, *Jesus and the Twelve* (Downers Grove, IL: InterVarsity; Leicester: Apollos, 2004), 177–206.

4. H. G. M. Williamson, "Samaritans," *Dictionary of Jesus and the Gospels*, ed. Joel B. Green, Scott McKnight, and I. Howard Marshall (Downers Grove, IL: InterVarsity, 1992), 724–28; Robert T. Anderson and Terry Giles, *The Keepers: An Introduction to the History and Culture of the Samaritans* (Grand Rapids: Baker Academic, 2001); cf. J. Massyngberde Ford, *My Enemy Is My Guest: Jesus and Violence in Luke* (Maryknoll, NY: Orbis, 1984), 80–86.

5. Schnabel, *Early Christian Mission*, 1:242–47, 260–62.

6. D. A. Carson, *The Gospel according to John* (Leicester: Inter-Varsity; Grand Rapids: Eerdmans, 1991), 215–16; Bock and Herrick, *Jesus in Context*, 211–12.

7. Bock and Herrick, *Jesus in Context*, 212.

8. Darrell L. Bock, *Luke, vol. 2*, Baker Exegetical Commentary on the New Testament (Grand Rapids: Baker Academic, 1996), 1405–6.

9. Craig L. Blomberg, *Interpreting the Parables*, 2nd ed. (Downers Grove, IL: InterVarsity, 2012), 295–302; cf. Bock, *Luke, vol. 2*, 1018–35; Ford, *My Enemy Is My Guest*, 91–94.

10. In terms of the Old Testament, note, for instance: the sheep and goats (Ezek. 34:17), the Son of Man (Dan. 7), coming with the angels (Zech. 14:5). For details, see Keener, *Commentary on the Gospel of Matthew*, 602–4; Bock and Herrick, *Jesus in Context*, 183–85.

11. Ivor H. Jones, *The Matthean Parables: A Literary and Historical Commentary*, Novum Testamentum Supplements 80 (Leiden: Brill, 1995), 246–49; W. D. Davies and Dale C. Allison, *A Critical and Exegetical Commentary on the Gospel of Saint Matthew*, International Critical Commentary (Edinburgh: T&T Clark, 1997), 3:422–23; cf. Ernesto Cardenal, "The Last Judgment (Matt. 25:31–46)," in *The Gospel in Solentiname*, trans. Donald D. Walsh (Maryknoll, NY: Orbis, 1982), 4:49–60.

12. For "little ones" and "the least" (the superlative of "little ones"), see Matt. 5:19; 10:42; 11:11; 18:6, 10, 14. For "brothers and sisters" as disciples, see 5:22–24, 47; 7:3–5; 12:48–50; 18:15, 21, 35; 23:8; 28:10; as Jesus's siblings, see 12:46–47; 13:55; as the siblings of others, see 1:2, 11; 4:18, 21; 10:2, 21; 14:3; 17:1; 19:29; 20:24–25.

13. Craig L. Blomberg, *Matthew*, New American Commentary 22 (Nashville: Broadman & Holman, 1992), 377–80; Keener, *Commentary on the Gospel of Matthew*, 604–6.

14. Note Aquiles Ernesto Martínez in "Jesus, the Immigrant Child: A Diasporic Reading of Matthew 2:1–23," *Apuntes* 26, no. 3 (2006): 84–114; Ched Myers and Matthew Colwell, *Our God Is Undocumented: Biblical Faith and Immigrant Justice* (St. Louis: Chalice, 2012), 159–77.

15. In his article "The Least of These My Brothers: Matthew 25:31–46" (*Apuntes* 23, no. 3 [2003]: 100–109), David Cortés-Fuentes despairs that there is no direct correlation to the Hispanic community and concludes that they cannot

wait for the majority culture to help; they must take the initiative to take care of themselves. I believe that he has missed the potential application of the passage and the thrust of the Bible in general.

16. There are many sources one could cite. Of those already mentioned, see especially Blomberg, *Jesus and the Gospels*; cf. Scot McKnight, *A New Vision for Israel: The Teachings of Jesus in National Context* (Grand Rapids: Eerdmans, 1999), 156–237. Willard M. Swartley places the Samaritan issue within Jesus's vision of peace and peacemaking in *Covenant of Peace: The Missing Peace in New Testament Theology and Ethics* (Grand Rapids: Eerdmans, 2006), 140–44 (Luke 10), 304–23 (John 4).

17. For this vocabulary and how the Septuagint (the Greek translation of the Hebrew text) rendered the Hebrew terminology, see K. L. Schmidt, M. A. Schmidt, and R. Meyer, "*paroikos*," in *Theological Dictionary of the New Testament*, ed. Gerhard Friedrich, trans. Geoffrey W. Bromiley (Grand Rapids: Eerdmans, 1967), 5:841–53; H. Bietenhard and F. S. Rothenberg, "Foreign, Alien, Dispersion, Stranger," in Brown, *New International Dictionary of New Testament Theology*, 1:683–92. Extensive discussions are found in John H. Elliott, *A Home for the Homeless: A Sociological Exegesis of 1 Peter, Its Situation and Strategy* (Minneapolis: Fortress, 1990), 21–36; and Elliott, *1 Peter*, Anchor Bible 37B (New York: Doubleday, 2000), 476–83.

18. Those who argue for some kind of sociopolitical explanation, although with distinct reconstructions, include Elliott (*Home for the Homeless*, 37–100; *1 Peter*, passim) and Karen H. Jobes, *1 Peter*, Baker Exegetical Commentary on the New Testament (Grand Rapids: Baker Academic, 2005), 28–42, 61–66. The spiritual explanation is presented by Thomas R. Schreiner, *1, 2 Peter, Jude*, New American Commentary 37 (Nashville: Broadman & Holman, 2003), 37–41.

19. See, e.g., Benjamin H. Dunning, *Aliens and Sojourners: Self as Other in Early Christianity*, Divinations: Reading Later Ancient Religion (Philadelphia: University of Pennsylvania Press, 2009).

20. Christine D. Pohl, *Making Room: Recovering Hospitality as a Christian Tradition* (Grand Rapids: Eerdmans, 1999); "Biblical Issues in Mission and Migration," *Missiology: An International Review* 31, no. 1 (2003): 3–15; "Responding to Strangers: Insights from the Christian Tradition," *Studies in Christian Ethics* 19, no. 1 (2006): 81–101. For an exegetical approach, see Arterbury, *Entertaining Angels*.

21. In her publications, Pohl also highlights Matt. 25:31–46. This text has been important in reflections on Christian hospitality to all, even if exegetically the reach of the biblical text is more limited.

22. Daniel G. Groody, "Fruit of the Vine and Work of Human Hands: Immigration and the Eucharist," in *A Promised Land, A Perilous Journey: Theological Perspectives on Migration*, ed. D. G. Groody and G. Campese (Notre Dame: University of Notre Dame Press, 2008), 299–315; Craig Wong, "The Table That Turns Us: How the Lord's Supper Changes the Immigration Conversation," in *Thinking Christianly about Immigration*, ed. M. Daniel Carroll R., Grounds Institute of Public Ethics Monograph Series 4 (Littleton: Denver Seminary, 2011), 25–42.

23. In the first edition of this book I deliberately kept my comments on Romans 13 brief. Too much attention had been placed on the passage to the neglect of the rest of the Bible. My strategy to focus on other parts of Scripture was misinterpreted as a "dismissive treatment" of the passage (Hoffmeier, *The Immigration*

Crisis, 144). Hoffmeier argues that there is nothing in the New Testament—and the rest of the Bible—that would put into question US immigration law (131–52).

24. The most extensive theological treatment that I have found of this tension with regard to immigration is *Immigrants among Us: A Lutheran Framework for Addressing Immigration Issues*, A Report of the Commission on Theology and Church Relations, The Lutheran Church—Missouri Synod (St. Louis: Concordia, 2012). This report is also available in Spanish. For a different Lutheran reflection, see Peter C. Meilander, *Toward a Theory of Immigration* (New York: Palgrave, 2001).

Chapter 5: Where Do We Go from Here?

1. Stanley Hauerwas and William H. Willimon, *Resident Aliens: Life in the Christian Colony; A Provocative Christian Assessment of Culture and Ministry for People Who Know That Something Is Wrong* (Nashville: Abingdon, 1989); cf. Stanley Hauerwas, *In Good Company: The Church as Polis* (Notre Dame: University of Notre Dame Press, 1995).

2. I have applied some of Hauerwas's insights to the immigration debate elsewhere. See M. Daniel Carroll R., "The Bible, the Church, and Human Rights in Contemporary Debates about Hispanic Immigration in the United States," *Journal of Latin American Theology* 2, no. 1 (2007): 161–84.

3. Richard S. Briggs, *The Virtuous Reader: Old Testament Narrative and Interpretive Virtue*, Studies in Theological Interpretation (Grand Rapids: Baker Academic, 2010).

4. In what follows I am indebted to Miroslav Volf, *Exclusion and Embrace: A Theological Exploration of Identity, Otherness, and Reconciliation* (Nashville: Abingdon, 1996). For his discussion of "soft embrace," see pp. 140–47.

Appendix

1. A number of universities have immigration research centers. Examples are the University of California–San Diego Center for Comparative Immigration Studies (www.ccis-ucsd.org) and the University of Notre Dame's Institute for Latino Studies (www.nd.edu/~latino). Another source of information is the Chicano and Latino/a departments in universities nationwide.

Index